DISCRIMINATION AND CONGRESSIONAL CAMPAIGN CONTRIBUTIONS

Discrimination and Congressional Campaign Contributions

JOHN THEILMANN
AND
AL WILHITE

PRAEGER

New York
Westport, Connecticut
London

Library of Congress Cataloging-in-Publication Data

Theilmann, John M. (John Meier)
Discrimination and congressional campaign contributions / John
Theilmann and Al Wilhite.
p. cm.
Includes bibliographical references and index.
ISBN 0–275–93695–3 (alk. paper)
1. Campaign funds—United States. 2. United States. Congress—
Elections. 3. Afro-American politicians—United States. 4. Women
in politics—United States. 5. Race discrimination—United States.
6. Sex discrimination—United States. I. Wilhite, Al. II. Title.
JK1991.T49   1991
324.7'8'0973—dc20   91–8298

British Library Cataloguing in Publication Data is available.

Library of Congress Catalog Card Number: 91–8298
ISBN: 0–275–93695–3

First published in 1991

Praeger Publishers, One Madison Avenue, New York, NY   10010
An imprint of Greenwood Publishing Group, Inc.

Printed in the United States of America

The paper used in this book complies with the
Permanent Paper Standard issued by the National
Information Standards Organization (Z39.48–1984).

10 9 8 7 6 5 4 3 2 1

Contents

Preface

Racism and sexism are emotionally charged issues; they are issues that demand political attention. Evidence that blacks and women are gaining political influence is reflected in the growing number of public offices they now occupy. Blacks and women have far more political clout today than even ten years ago. In the face of this success, however, is the plodding rate of change at the national level. There are proportionally far fewer women and blacks in Congress than in the U.S. population. This disproportionate representation has historical, cultural, psychological, and political roots, and its perpetuation defies simple explanation. This study investigates a single aspect of the underrepresentation problem: the role of money. Money has been part of the electoral process since before the Revolution, and its role in the current makeup of Congress should be understood. Every day there seems to be more voices clamoring for the diminution of money's influence on Capitol Hill. This is a change that could remake the face of Congress and the position of women and blacks in that body.

This study focuses on the influence of money on the election of black and female candidates to the House of Representatives. Implicit is a concern with representation and the impact of campaign contributions on congressional elections in general. The decade of the eighties has been a transition period in campaign financing and in the election of women and blacks to public office. By the end of the decade, women and blacks were being elected to public office in increasingly larger numbers, and even when they lost, they were treated as creditable candidates. By the decade's close, political changes wrought by the Federal Election Campaign Act (FECA) of 1974 were coming under fire from several camps. Nonetheless, defenders point out that the situation is far improved over the past and may be superior to some of the suggested reforms. In any case, the scent of reform is in the air; it is an opportune time to ponder the past.

Money has an impact on the electability of all congressional candidates, especially challengers and candidates for open seats, but not all candidates compete on a level playing field when it comes to campaign finances. Some, particularly incumbents, have access to huge sums, while others must make do with scant resources. Because the United States is not a race- or gender-blind society, funding sources may consider a candidate's race and/or gender in making contribution decisions. It is this consideration we test.

The political situation of the 1980s should not be examined in isolation from earlier developments as today's climate has evolved over centuries. Hence, the first two chapters provide a historical overview of the changing political outlook for blacks and women in the United States. Chapter 1 is a brief examination of the political position of women and blacks from the early years of the Republic to the 1970s. Chapter 2 examines the notable political gains made by both groups during the seventies. One route blacks and women have traveled to reach their political goals is the pursuit of public office. This topic is of particular concern in chapter 2. The third chapter provides a historical overview of the impact of political money and focuses on several explanations of the role of money in congressional elections since the passage of the FECA.

The next four chapters are theoretical explorations of campaign decisions linked with empirical measures of the influence of race and gender on these decisions. Chapter 4 presents a rent-seeking model of the campaign strategy. This approach enables us to construct a rigorous explanation of both candidate and contributor decisions. The theoretical perspective developed in this chapter will then serve as the basis for analysis of political action contributions (chapter 5), party contributions (chapter 6), and individual contributions (chapter 7).

In the last chapter we return to the question of blacks and women in Congress as impacted by campaign funding. Based on our analysis we make some predictions for the future for black and female congressional candidates.

Our approach is in part historical/narrative and in part theoretical/statistical. A historical perspective places the threads of today's world in a larger fabric, while a theoretical/quantitative approach allows us to focus. Because we blend the perspectives of two disciplines, specialists from each may become impatient with our discussion. On occasion we will seem too simplistic and abstract for some political scientists, and other times we will be too pragmatic for some economists. In each case we ask the reader's indulgence.

One means of examining the impact of campaign finances on congressional campaigns is through the use of interview data. We do not rely on this methodology. Instead, we concentrate on rigorous theoretical models and statistical measures of contributions. There are two advantages to this approach. First, financial data are more amenable to statistical manipulation than are interview data. Second, the nature of the question we wish to pursue, discrimination, is likely to bias survey data. For example, how would a PAC director respond to the question, "Do you discriminate?" Even an honest negative answer could mask unintentional discrimination.

In short, we are not concerned with contributors', voters', and candidates' opinions about discrimination, nor are we concerned with the myriad of prejudicial forces at work. Instead, we pursue a simple tale, picking up clues by examining the outcome.

In studies of gender-related issues, prudence dictates avoiding the use of value-laden terminology. Because we refer to individual candidate's decisions, we have adopted the use of alternating female and male pronouns when referring to members of Congress rather than the cumbersome he/she assemblage. The exception is in our discussion of the nineteenth century, when all House members were male.

This is a work of joint authorship. Both authors have contributed and share responsibility for the strengths and weaknesses of the whole.

DISCRIMINATION AND CONGRESSIONAL CAMPAIGN CONTRIBUTIONS

Chapter One

Representation: Blacks and Women in the Political Process

The right of citizens of the United States to vote shall not be denied or abridged by the United States or by any State on account of race, color, or previous condition of servitude.

Amendment XV (1870)

The right of citizens of the United States to vote shall not be denied or abridged by the United States or by any State on account of sex.

Amendment XIX (1920)

Democractic governance wears many guises, each possessing its own distribution of rewards and responsibilities. The evolution of democracy in the United States has included a broadening of the electorate. The Fifteenth and Nineteenth amendments represent two large changes, and democratic theorists and scholars agree in general that these expansions have had a positive effect on the political process. Enabling women and blacks to vote is, however, only part of the story. Voting does not mean a group has become a full member of the decision-making structure. Blacks and women have been part of the political calculus for some time on one level, that of voting, but on another level their participation has been sharply circumscribed. Political participation also involves running for and holding office at all levels. Local officeholding is an important means of fostering political consciousness, gaining political experience, and influencing and making public policy. Members of Congress are part of a national political elite, and as such possess access to policymaking at the national level.

In this chapter we look briefly at the question of representation and then review the historical background of black and female suffrage and the first entry of these groups into congressional officeholding. In this context we examine reasons for the initial exclusion of these groups as well as identify the first halting steps made to include them in the electorate. The tale for this chapter concludes in 1970.

The 1970s are a watershed in both racial and sexual politics in the United States. By the early seventies federal legislation had opened the way for increased black political participation. The underrepresentation of blacks in Congress was also becoming of some concern to democratic theorists. The women's movement, too, was gaining a foothold in the political consciousness of Americans. Although an equal rights amendment was first introduced in Congress in 1923 and was reintroduced in every subsequent legislative session, it did not pass both houses of Congress until 1972. Chapter 2 builds on the foundation laid here to examine the growth in the number of women and blacks in Congress in the seventies and eighties.

WHAT IS REPRESENTATION?

This study is broadly concerned with the question of representation for blacks and women in Congress. Political participation of blacks and women does not guarantee representation in Congress, and so the complex concept of representation requires exploration. While definitions of representation abound, there seem to be four major meanings of the term.[1] The simplest is descriptive representation, which emphasizes the physical characteristics of the representative. A representative who is of the same sex and/or race as her constituents represents them in one fashion. In another, more-important form, their policy views, she may not represent them at all. The second sort of representation emphasizes that a representative's policy views match those of his constituency (see Eulau and Karps 1977). In this instance the representative votes in accordance with the views of the majority of his constituents. However, determining the views of the majority may often be problematic. A third theory of representation focuses on the congruence of the views of the electorate and the representative body as a whole. Here, representation is achieved if the views of a constituency are represented by some members of the legislative body, even if not by their own representatives (see Weisberg 1978, Hurley 1982). This sort of representation captures, for example, the person in Texas who contributes to the re-election campaign of a congressman from North Carolina because he votes in support of issues of concern to the Texan. The fourth form of representation is that of acting on behalf of others. The representative is an independent agent in this case who makes decisions about what is best for her constituents even if it does not directly coincide with the wishes of the constituency.[2] Hanna Pitkin provides one of the clearest modern expressions of this perception:

> Representing here means acting in the interest of the represented, in a manner responsive to them. The representative must act independently; his action must involve discretion and judgment; he must be the one who acts. He must not be found persistently at odds with the wishes of the represented without good reason in terms of their interest, without a good explanation of why their wishes are not in accord with their interest. (Pitkin 1967, 209–10)

In essence, the last three theories of representation describe substantive as opposed to descriptive representation. These three theories emphasize the policy views of the represented and the representative. The importance of the first theory of representation is based on the necessity first to obtain descriptive representation in order to gain substantive representation.

An illustration of the substantive conception of representation would be a white male congressman who voted for the Voting Rights Act of 1965 or the Equal Rights Amendment. In neither case did he have the same physical characteristics as some of his constituents, but he voted in such a way as to reflect their views. Another example would be a female state legislator who voted against the adoption of the Equal Rights Amendment, giving the reason that a positive vote would be harmful to her constituents. Without shared policy goals, descriptive representation is not genuine representation. Kenneth Prewitt and Heinz Eulau describe the third definition as they emphasize the collective nature of representation. They understand representation to be a "relationship between two collectives—the representative assembly and the represented citizenry" (1969, 428). If Prewitt and Eulau's *caveat* is adopted, then descriptive and substantive representation can be joined, as Congress is seen as balancing the interests of voters in all congressional districts. While this definition is less apt for Congress than it is for the city councils to which Prewitt and Eulau apply it, it has bearing here.

Arguments running counter to an emphasis on solely substantive representation concern black and female representation as they point out the importance of physical characteristics of a representative. These views take the attitudinal argument into account by maintaining that a larger number of female and black officeholders is not sufficient to enhance the representation of women and blacks, but that it is necessary to ensure its occurrence. Virginia Sapiro (1981), for example, contends that an increased number of women in office has made government more responsive to women's interests as well as ensuring a more equitable distribution of political power. This same argument can also be made concerning black officeholders. Charles Bullock (1981; see also Combs, Hibbing, and Welch 1984, and Whitby 1987) indirectly weakens this argument in pointing out that the southern Democratic congressional delegation, which was almost exclusively white in the 1970s, became more responsive to the needs of their black constituents simply because those constituents were able to vote. Another reason for the election of blacks and women is the symbolic value of their position as officeholders. Evidence for this is sketchy at best, although F. Glenn Abney (1974) found black political participation to be related to the presence of black candidates on the ballot, and more recently Jesse Jackson's presidential candidacy has increased black turnout. Lawrence Bobo and Franklin Gilliam (1990) also find that in some areas, particularly with city councils and mayorships in which blacks are empowered, they participate more than do whites of comparable socioeconomic status. Presence on the ballot is not, however, the same as representation, since running for office is not the same as holding office. Nonetheless, increasing the numbers of female and black officeholders increases their acceptability in government. Finally, there may be some issues on which female and black representatives represent the issues of their female and black constitutents better than do white males. As Susan Carroll puts it: "Women's interests on policy issues dealing with women have not been adequately represented by governing bodies" (1985, 20). Black citizens may also feel black elected officials represent their concerns better than do white officials.

The question of the representation of women and blacks is made more complex by the distribution of the population. Women constitute more than 50 percent of the U.S. population and are found in this ratio in almost every congressional district. Blacks make up 12 percent of the population but tend to be concentrated in specific areas. In the sense conceptualized by the first and third definitions of representation, a black congressman from Chicago could represent a black person in Montana, but a representative is generally regarded as being responsible to the consitutents of his district. During the 1950s Adam Clayton Powell of New York often seemed to be taking this symbolic broader approach as he tried to serve as a spokesman for blacks nationwide with his attacks on segregation. Black representation thus poses a problem not found in connection with female representation. Achieving demographic representation for blacks may be harder to achieve than it is for women.

Achieving demographic representation takes us to the heart of the representation question. Does a member of Congress represent the voters of her district, her contributors, or her ethnic or gender group? The standard answer is that a representative represents all the people of a district. The counterevidence is that southern congressmen did not represent their black constituents very well until the 1970s, or that male congressmen have not always represented the wishes of their female constituents. Simply electing blacks or women does not totally alleviate the problem. What then of white males? Or, can a black man represent black women? What about Hispanics or Asian-Americans? The combinations quickly become endless, and the ensuing complications quickly reach absurdity. The obvious answer is to abandon the whole mess and conclude that representatives represent their districts, period. This, too, begs the question because it does not ensure responsive representation—a prerequisite of any definition. Moreover, Congress is expected, at least to some extent, to try to achieve goals that are satisfactory to all citizens, not just those in individual districts.

What is at issue with the number of female and black members of Congress is not a pure representation question. In spite of the views of some commentators (e.g., Sapiro 1981, Baxter and Lansing 1983, Darcy, Welch, and Clarke 1987), increasing the number of black and female representatives and senators would not guarantee "better" representation for these groups in Congress; the election of candidates sympathetic to their goals would. If it is assumed that black and female candidates are more likely than are white males to be sympathetic to black and female policy goals, then the election of increased numbers of women and blacks is important. We will return to the representation question again in the last chapter after gleaning some specific information to add to this discussion.

BLACK AND WOMEN SUFFRAGE

Before the question of electing women and blacks to Congress can be specifically addressed, we must turn to the issue of suffrage. The rest of this chapter considers how women and blacks gained the vote and how it was translated into representation in the years before 1970.

The early U.S. Republic was not based on ideas of equality as we define them today. The framers of the Constitution intended government to be conducted by the "best men," that is, well-educated men with an economic stake in the country. This definition excluded women, blacks, Indians, and often the poor. Slaves were excluded from political participation by their status. Women and free blacks were not inherently incapable of political participation, but in fact they were not allowed to vote or hold office.

There were exceptions to this generalization, to be sure. In New Jersey, women and free blacks gained voting rights in local and congressional elections based on the state constitution of 1776. The New Jersey constitution had defined voters loosely as "all free inhabitants" of the state, an oversight enabling free blacks and women to exercise voting rights. The legislature disenfranchised both groups in 1807 on the grounds that their votes could be easily manipulated. This fear of political corruption continued to be cited throughout the nineteenth century as a reason for excluding blacks, women, and the poor from the electoral process.

The attitude that women and blacks were not suitable participants in the political process persisted well into the twentieth century. The tide gradually turned against slavery, but many abolitionists did not take the next step and accept black equality. There were also hardy advocates of equality for women in the early nineteenth century, but their advocacy bore scant fruit. Both blacks and women seemed doomed to remain entirely excluded from the political process in the first half of the nineteenth century.

There were, however, signs of change. States relaxed suffrage restrictions for white males over time, and by 1850 white males were full participants in the political process. Abolitionism gained ground in the North, although southern opposition to the abolition of slavery hardened apace. Some blacks and women recognized their common position and sought to join forces. Particularly in the North an alliance was forged in the 1840s between abolitionists and supporters of women's suffrage. Some women, such as the Charlestonians Angelina and Sarah Grimke, specifically linked the plight of the two. Some abolitionists, such as William Lloyd Garrison and former slave Frederick Douglass, supported voting rights for women. The Women's Rights Convention at Seneca Falls, New York, in 1848 was the most forthright attack on male dominance and called for women's suffrage to right these wrongs. Abolitionists were also present at Seneca Falls, and the two movements seemed to be moving toward a common goal. Yet there were always forces at work to pry the alliance apart. Southern women, with a few exceptions such as the Grimke sisters, were ambivalent when it came to opposing slavery and advocating suffrage for women (Scott 1970). Even though they might see some parallels between slaves and their own position, the racial overtones of slavery helped to prevent criticism of the institution. Also in the South, defenders of slavery often tied its preservation to an opposition to women's rights. The linking of female and black rights could thus have a negative as well as a positive impact on achieving suffrage for either group.

Abolitionists rather than feminists had the first successes. President Lincoln saw the Civil War as a struggle to preserve the Union, yet he gradually came to link it to the destruction of slavery. The Emancipation Proclamation, a wartime expedient issued in September 1862, started the process but did not provide for universal emancipation. Instead, Lincoln ordered the freeing of slaves in the Confederate states still in rebellion. The Emancipation Proclamation freed few slaves and left the legal position and citizenship of the freed slaves in limbo, but it was a superb moral gesture. Lincoln's ambiguity gradually turned to certainty; he advocated in the Republican National Convention in 1864 a constitutional amendment banning slavery, and later lobbied Congress on its behalf. His stand is clouded by the negotiations that he and Secretary of State Seward carried out with three Confederate commissioners at Hampton Roads in February 1865. Lincoln seems to have been trying to appeal to southern Whigs in the postwar era, an appeal that was couched in terms of toleration for southern institutions.

Lincoln's position at the Hampton Roads Conference was that the southern states should be quickly readmitted to the Union so that they would be allowed to vote on the ratification of the Thirteenth Amendment. Moreover, he spoke in terms of gradual, compensated emancipation at Hampton Roads. In spite of his personal hatred of slavery, the president's official position was more ambivalent. Nonetheless, emancipation was in the air. Jefferson Davis, the Confederate president, also came out in favor of emancipation in fall 1864. Davis's plan was to use slaves to alleviate the manpower shortage of the South. In return, the men who joined the Confederate Army and their families were to be freed.

Whatever Lincoln's plan, his assassination in April 1865 left Reconstruction in the hands of Andrew Johnson and increasingly in the hands of congressional leaders such as senators Charles Sumner and Ben Wade and Representative Thaddeus Stevens. Congressional Reconstruction had many goals, but one was to gain a measure of political equality for blacks.

Reconstruction brought great changes to the status of black Americans. The adoption of the Thirteenth Amendment in 1865 pointed the way by banning slavery. Banning slavery did not guarantee equality for blacks, nor even suffrage, and southern states quickly took measures to ensure that the former slaves would live in a status similar to slavery. The congressional response was not slow in coming. Military occupation helped to protect southern blacks from intimidation. The Freedman's Bureau tried to provide educational opportunites for the largely uneducated black population of the southern states. The Fourteenth Amendment (ratified in 1868) encapsulated the spirit of the congressional plan of Reconstruction. It nullified the Confederate war debt and prohibited former Confederate leaders from returning to Congress. More important, in the long run it clearly acknowledged that blacks were citizens and that all citizens were entitled to equal protection under the law. Furthermore, no citizen could be denied the basic rights of life, liberty, and property without due process under the law. In time the courts used these clauses of the Fourteenth Amendment to extend basic rights to all Americans. Congress followed this with the passage of another constitutional amendment in 1869 specifically guaranteeing voting rights for blacks. Southern legislatures bitterly resented both the Fourteenth and Fifteenth amendments, but in the end they had to accede to them as the price of readmission to the Union. Protecting voting rights for blacks also met with resistance in the North, and it took the reluctant votes of four southern states to ratify the Fifteenth Amendment in 1870.

Reconstruction improved the status of blacks throughout the country, although they remained far from equal. Black political participation led to some impressive gains in the South, but blacks achieved a majority only in the lower house of the South Carolina legislature. At the state level, blacks were elected to a variety of posts but never to a governorship during Reconstruction. Between 1865 and 1877 sixteen blacks were elected to Congress (fourteen in the House and two in the Senate). Mississippi even sent two black senators to Washington: Blanche Bruce and Hiram Revels. South Carolina sent Joseph Rainey to Congress for five terms from 1871 to 1879. The end of Reconstruction in 1877 did not spell the end of black political participation in the South as blacks served in Congress for every term save one (the Fiftieth Congress) until 1901. All told, twenty black representatives and two senators (all Republicans) served in Congress from 1870 to 1901. Only three of the eleven former Confederate states, Texas, Arkansas, and Tennessee, had not sent a black to Congress before the turn of the century, while South Carolina sent the most (eight). Nonetheless, through a program of legal restrictions and extralegal terrorism, blacks were discouraged from exercising their voting rights. The Mississippi legislature, for example, redrew the boundaries of John Lynch's district in 1876 so it stretched for 500 miles across the state while it was only 40 miles wide (Parker 1984). By the mid-1890s white supremacists controlled the political process in the South and excluded almost all blacks from the electoral process. George White gained election in North Carolina in 1896, serving two terms in Congress. In 1900, he saw the handwriting on the wall and declined to seek re-election. In his valedictory speech to the House on January 29, 1901, in support of an antilynching bill, he called for equal treatment for blacks, sitting down to prolonged applause (Christopher 1976). It was twenty-eight years before another black representative took a seat in Congress.

Nineteenth-century black congressmen seem to have met the standards for all four definitions of representation. Since their districts had majority black populations, they fit the descriptive model of representation. Moreover, they tried to match the policy preferences of the majority of their constitutents. Most even saw themselves as acting for their con-stitutents, even those whites who opposed black rights, as they argued that the political integration of blacks was necessary for the well being of southern society. Black congressmen also gave real and symbolic representation to blacks elsewhere in the country. Only if the views of black congressmen are balanced against those of the South as a whole is their representation questionable. Unfortunately a majority of Americans (especially southerners) were disinclined to expand the rights of black citizens beyond a bare minimum in the nineteenth century.

Even though Reconstruction opened up the political process to black men, women were not yet included, and in some ways black enfranchise-ment drove a wedge between the former allies. Because Congress extended voting rights to black men, but not white women, some southerners raised the specter of black domination of white women. Occupied with defending their newly acquired status, many black leaders could not devote a great deal of attention to trying to aid their former allies. Many white women resented their continuing disenfranchisement and set out to gain the vote on their own. After that, many were disinclined to defend black political rights.

A referenda campaign in Kansas in 1867 is indicative of the split between abolitionists and women. In March 1867, the Kansas legislature authorized two separate issues to be presented to the voters that fall: black suffrage and women suffrage. The campaign resulted in bitter charges and countercharges and both issues went down to defeat (DuBois 1978).

The wedge that had been placed between former allies by the Fourteenth Amendment was now driven home, shattering the American Equal Rights Association, which had been formed in 1866, as women began to go their own way. The debate among suffragists over the role of the Republican party in achieving voting rights for women expanded into a debate over the ratification of the Fifteenth Amendment. Some leaders, such as Susan B. Anthony and Elizabeth Cady Stanton, denounced the amendment because it ignored women, while others preferred to look to the Republican party for future assistance. The upshot was the formation of two national organizations, the American Woman Suffrage Association and the National Woman Suffrage Association (DuBois 1978). Both groups continued to work to achieve a ballot for women although employing somewhat different tactics.

This is not to say that women were completely disenfranchised in the Reconstruction era. In 1838, Kentucky extended the right to vote for local school boards to widows. Kansas granted the right to vote for school boards to all women in 1859. In the 1870s a Missouri couple, Francis and Virginia Minor, with support from the National Woman Suffrage Association, sued a St. Louis registrar who had refused to allow Virginia to vote. The Minors argued that the Fourteenth Amendment protected the rights of all Americans, including women. The Supreme Court heard the case in 1875 after a series of adverse decisions in lower courts. The Court's decision, which upheld the lower courts' rulings, was that suffrage did not automatically accompany citizenship and that states could legally withhold voting rights from certain classes of citizens such as women.

The fight for women's suffrage was now joined. One of the movement's indomitable leaders was Susan B. Anthony, who also tried and failed to vote in 1872. By 1878 she and Elizabeth Cady Stanton had convinced Senator A. A. Sargent of California to introduce a constitutional amendment that said: "The right of citizens of the United States to vote shall not be denied or abridged by the United States or any State on account of sex." When the Nineteenth Amendment granting women the vote was ratified in 1920, it contained these same words. Suffragists fought the struggle for women's suffrage on two fronts in the latter half of the nineteenth century. The National Woman Suffrage Association led the movement to gain women's suffrage at the national level, while the American Woman Suffrage Association worked for constitutional amendments at the state level. In 1890 the two groups merged into the National American Woman Suffrage Association in order to project a broad-based effort.

In spite of the efforts of these and other groups, women acquired the vote at a glacial pace. From 1870 to 1910, seventeen states (eleven of them west of the Mississippi) held referenda on women's suffrage with most denying it. Even so, the movement gained new adherents as more women became interested in politics. By 1890, three states allowed women to vote on tax and bond issues, and nineteen had granted the vote on school issues. Particularly with school issues, the tie to the home, a traditional women's sphere, was manifest so men were more inclined to allow the expression of a feminine viewpoint.

Antisuffrage sentiment remained strong in the late nineteenth century; it too was tied to the home, often taking divine inspiration for excluding women from the political arena. Ex-president Grover Cleveland maintained in 1905 that God had decreed the division of labor between men and women with men to play a role in the public arena and women to stay at home and bear and raise children (Kraditor 1965). Other antisuffragists argued that women were biologically incapable of exercising the franchise, so that enfranchising women would lead to "improper" voting. They followed this calumny by contending that most women did not want the vote anyway. In reality, antisuffragism had no coherent ideology save a vague conception of the inferiority of women; it responded to the suffragists' arguments as they arose and was not always consistent in its own arguments (Kraditor 1965).

In 1890, Wyoming took the first step toward a wider form of participation for women when it entered the Union with a constitution that granted equal voting rights to women and men.[3] Colorado followed suit in 1893, as did Idaho and Utah in 1896. Thereafter, it was another fourteen years before another state extended equal suffrage to women. During the Progressive Era, the drive for women's suffrage gained momentum partially because supporters argued that enfranchising women would lead to "clean" government, yet it ran against a stone wall of opposition founded on traditional views of women in some parts of the country, most notably the South and Midwest. The drive for obtaining the vote on a state-by-state basis seemed doomed to failure.

During the second decade of the twentieth century suffragists shifted emphasis to the national level. Congress responded and in June 1919 passed the Nineteenth Amendment granting voting rights to women, and the necessary thirty-two states ratified it by August 1920. Women had gained the vote, but this did not lead to a great influx of women into public office. One woman, Jeanette Rankin of Montana, had already been elected to the House of Representatives in 1916. In 1922 Mae Nolan succeeded her husband in office and served out the term to which he had been reelected (Gertzog 1984). Nolan, unlike Rankin, seemed to be a role model for many future women members of Congress, those who succeeded their husbands in office. As Irwin Gertzog (1984) points out, from 1927 to 1944 at least half of all female representatives succeeded their husbands in the House.

As women began to make political gains in the 1890s, blacks began to be driven from the political arena in the South. In the North, blacks retained the status quo of voting but were otherwise regarded as second-class citizens. Violence of one sort or another had long been used to keep southern blacks "in their place," but in the nineties, white supremacists also applied the force of law. In 1896 the Supreme Court sanctioned "separate but equal" facilities in *Plessy* v. *Ferguson*, which led to the exclusion of blacks from public transportation, public parks, restrooms, and the like. The era of Jim Crow had arrived in the South, supported by northern opinion and the federal courts. Black suffrage soon followed other rights into decline.[4] In 1898 the Supreme Court upheld the Mississippi plan for disenfranchising blacks through literacy tests in *Williams* v. *Mississippi*. Literacy tests were joined to poll taxes and ultimately the whites-only primary to exclude almost completely blacks from political participation in the South in following years. In Louisiana, for example, 130,444 blacks were registered to vote in 1897, which was 44 percent of the electorate. A new state constitution, which included various restrictions on suffrage, reduced this number to 5,320, or 4.1 percent of the electorate, by 1900. By 1940 only .5 percent of the southern electorate was black (Walton, Jr. 1985, 86). The number of blacks registered to vote did not begin to creep upward until the 1940s when the Supreme Court disallowed the whites-only primary with *Smith* v. *Allright*. Not until the 1960s did blacks again take a political role in the South, and only then through intense outside pressure.

The 1928 elections brought the return of a black congressman to Washington with the election of Oscar DePriest of Chicago as the representative of the First District of Illinois. Like his predecessors, DePriest was a Republican, but his successor in the First District seat, Arthur Mitchell, who defeated DePriest in 1934, was a Democrat. The First District seat was held by black Democrats thereafter, including William Dawson, who served from 1943 to 1970, and later Harold Washington.

The election of first DePriest and then Mitchell signaled two important changes in the representation of black Americans. Prior to 1900, blacks had been elected to Congress from the South, but after 1928 they were elected from northern cities. Not until the election of Andrew Young from Atlanta in 1972 did a southern state send a black congressman to Congress. Initially blacks had been loyal to the party of Lincoln, but the New Deal and the rhetoric and actions of Franklin Roosevelt swayed many blacks into the Democratic column. After DePriest's loss in 1934 only Senator Edward Brooke from Massachusetts, who served from 1967 to 1979, was elected to Congress on the Republican ticket until the election of Gary Franks (CT 5) in 1990. Initially only one black congressman served in Washington, but in 1945 Adam Clayton Powell, Jr., of New York joined William Dawson in the House. Growth of the black delegation continued to be almost imperceptible. In 1955 a third black congressman joined the delegation, when Charles Diggs, Jr., went to Washington from Detroit. By 1960 the black delegation stood at five with the addition of John Conyers from Detroit, who joined Diggs, Powell, Dawson, and Robert Nix, who had been elected from a Philadelphia district in 1956.

During the 1960s a second Reconstruction began in the South, and it opened many doors to blacks. Legislation, such as the Voting Rights Act of 1965, attempted to ensure blacks the right to participate in the electoral process. Black registration figures went up dramatically during the sixties, as did white registration. For example, 6.9 percent of adult blacks in Mississippi were registered to vote in 1964, while in 1969, 66.5 percent were registered (Lawson 1976, 331). Similar changes occurred in other southern states, and by 1969, black registration figures had climbed substantially in the South even if they were still eclipsed by the number of whites registered to vote.

As with women, the legal right to participate did not carry with it an ability to be elected to office. Yet, by the mid-1970s some blacks had gained election to local offices in the South. Outside the South the situation was somewhat different as blacks increased their numbers in Congress and in local offices from several northern cities after World War II. A few, such as William Dawson of Chicago, even came to play a minor leadership role in the House. Northern black representatives came from urban areas such as New York, Chicago, and Detroit.

Once women gained the vote in 1920 there were no longer any legal barriers to their political participation, but subtle restraints remained. Particularly in the South the turnout rate of women remained below male turnout, but throughout the country women voted less and certainly ran for office less than men did between 1920 and 1960. World War II expanded the horizons of many women (and their husbands), and after the war women became more-active participants in the political process. Nonetheless, the ideal woman of the 1950s remained at home, concerning herself with child rearing. Such a goal might lead to election to a local school board, but few women considered a try for higher offices. For most voters the home, not the political arena, was a woman's province, and so they were disinclined to elect women to anything other than local office.[5] Although more women than blacks obtained congressional seats in the years after World War II, most played a small role in House deliberations, although notable exceptions existed, such as Leonor Sullivan from Missouri, who served from 1953 to 1977 and chaired the Merchant Marine and Fisheries Committee. Female representatives did not form as coherent a group in Congress as did black representatives since they came from both parties and often displayed different policy goals. Not all were even committed to further enhancing the political position of women. While their influence was diluted in Congress because they were from both parties, their increased numbers helped their chances for further political influence. Overall, by 1970, women had made far greater strides toward obtaining political power than had blacks.

The leaders of the civil rights movement of the 1960s directed their efforts primarily toward obtaining rights for black Americans, but women also made gains during the decade. Starting with their participation in the civil rights movement, some women began to demand increased political, social, and economic rights for themselves. Although these demands were not yet clearly focused at the end of the decade, the groundwork was laid that helped to break down some of the barriers to the election of women, just as the political gains of the sixties led to enhanced electoral opportunites for black candidates.

BLACKS AND WOMEN IN CONGRESS: THE EARLY YEARS

Political participation follows many routes, and an important avenue is running for and holding office. Election to Congress has a cachet of power to it that few other elective offices have. A governor may have more of a direct impact on people's lives, but membership in Congress connotes the ability to deal with national issues. This distinction is one argument for increasing black and female representation.

Before 1970, the number of women and blacks in Congress was low, and many obtained office under special circumstances. Black congressional membership even came to a halt at the turn of the century as a result of the restrictive electoral codes of the South. It resumed in 1928 with the election of Oscar DePriest from Illinois. By 1955 there were three blacks in Congress: William Dawson from Chicago, Adam Clayton

Powell from New York, and the newly elected Charles Diggs from Michigan. By 1965 the number had doubled, and in 1968 three more black representatives were elected. Ten blacks were elected to Congress in 1970, nine in the House and one, Edward Brooke of Massachusetts, in the Senate. With the exception of Brooke, all were Democrats, a New Deal legacy, and all came from urban areas. Even though they shared many of the same policy goals, their number was so low in the fifties as to limit them to informal meetings with no overall official agenda. The election of William Clay (Missouri), Louis Stokes (Ohio), and Shirley Chisholm (New York) in 1968 led to the formation of the group that would become the Democratic Select Committee and later the Congressional Black Caucus (Barnett 1982).

Although the number of black representatives increased during the sixties, their number was still low, and none came from the South, the region with the largest percentage of potential black voters. They were potential voters because only during the sixties did the number of eligible black voters in the South begin to reach significant numbers.

The second Reconstruction took two tracks: congressional and judicial action in Washington and grass-roots activity in the South. Although challenges to a segregated society began in earnest in the 1940s with the abolition of the whites-only primary in 1944 in *Smith* v. *Allright*, the bars to black voting did not begin to lift until the sixties. In 1964 the Twenty-Fourth Amendment was ratified, which outlawed the poll tax in federal elections. Also in that year the Civil Rights Act gave the Justice Department the power to guarantee voting rights in areas where it was circumscribed. The Voting Rights Act of 1965 specifically struck down barriers to black registration, including literacy tests, poll taxes in state and local elections, and racially discriminatory voting regulations.[6] The Voting Rights Act applied to all or parts of Alabama, Georgia, Louisiana, Mississippi, South Carolina, North Carolina, and Virginia; it was, as Earl and Merle Black put it, "the grand turning point in modern times for the reentry of black into southern politics (1987, 136)." The Johnson Administration worked hard to open up the political process to blacks in the South. In 1964 only one-fourth of the black population of the South was registered to vote, but by 1969 two-thirds of southern blacks were registered.

The increase in southern black political participation did not come about solely because of judicial and legislative action. Black and white activists throughout the South often risked their lives in order to help blacks to register and to vote. Efforts such as the Mississippi Summer Project of 1964 often were touched by violence and death.

Increased numbers of black voters did not, however, lead to the election of blacks to Congress. Increased black voting did produce a gradual increase in the number of local black officials throughout the South. Gerrymandering, the lack of experienced black candidates, and the slow pace of change in racial attitudes inhibited the election of blacks to Congress in the South.

Black congressional gains in the North in the 1960s were part of a general shift that led to increased political, civil, and economic rights. Yet as the decade drew to a close black Americans had a long way to go to achieve equality. Increasing the number of blacks in Congress still seemed to be one avenue to the achievement of this goal.

Women increased their numbers in Congress more quickly than blacks did even though they achieved voting rights later. The number of female elected officials remained low until the 1950s, and many in Congress arrived on their husbands' coattails, first filling unexpired terms that resulted from the death of their husbands. Most women representatives did not obtain leadership posts in the House, although a few gained secondary leadership roles (Gertzog 1984). During the fifties some women members began to be heard on national issues. Senator Margaret Chase Smith of Maine, for example, was one of the first senators to condemn the excesses of Senator Joseph McCarthy.

During the sixties another change relating to women in Congress was under way—more women were being elected in their own right rather than as the wives of former congressmen. Even so, the old avenue to Capitol Hill remained open—about one out of four new women elected to Congress between 1968 and 1975 were the widows of congressmen or congressional candidates (Thompson 1985). Even though women representatives became more assertive of their rights and demanded to be included in the inner circles of Congress, old attitudes died hard, and the congressional leadership remained a closed club of white males throughout the sixties. By the end of the seventies female representatives had formed the Congresswomen's Caucus as a means of enhancing their legislative clout in a bipartisan fashion and to help break down the bars of the male club atmosphere in Congress.[7]

There are many reasons for the failure of women to gain leadership status, such as a failure to gain seniority because many stayed only a few years, but one reason stems from geography. Just as southerners had been the most adamantly opposed to women's suffrage, they remained the most opposed to electing women to Congress or sharing political power with them. At least in the South women and blacks had something in common—their failure to be elected to Congress. The southern domination of Congress in the fifties, sixties, and early seventies also meant that a largely southern leadership of Congress was disinclined to share power with female members.

The civil rights movement ultimately had a positive impact on this gap. Many activists in the South were women, both black and white, but their early activism in behalf of blacks was rarely translated into electoral gains for themselves. Within the civil rights movement the prejudice of black males worked to disallow women a leadership role (Evans 1979), and northern women soon departed for home to pursue a career of activism there. This initial activism helped to widen the expectations of some voters concerning women's political abilities, making it easier for those women who did run for political office.

The civil rights movement had a positive aspect in another sense. It opened the door for the acquisition of equal rights by women. The Civil Rights Act of 1964 applied to both blacks and women.[8] The civil rights movement also led more women to become politically active, and some, especially some black women (Darcy and Hadley 1988) made the transition from action to running for office. The candidate pool was beginning to expand by the end of the decade. By 1970, electing more women to Congress was envisioned by some women as a way of furthering their efforts to gain equality.

By 1970, blacks and women had gained what neither had possessed at the beginning of the Republic: the right to vote. Members of both groups had been elected to Congress. But the number of representatives did not match the share of the population. What inhibited blacks and women from being elected to Congress? In both cases the obvious answer is their race or sex. But these characteristics did not totally exclude them from election.

In the past (and even today) black members of Congress have tended to be elected from districts with substantial black populations. Between 1870 and 1900, South Carolina, the state that elected the most black congressmen (eight), had a majority black population. By 1920, no southern state had a majority black population even though individual districts might still possess a black majority. As southern blacks moved north to cities such as Chicago or Detroit, they were initially represented by whites. This gradually began to change from 1928 onward. Even in 1970 there appeared to be a demographic threshold of at least a 30 percent black population for a black representative to be elected.

Nineteenth-century black congressmen exhibited many of the same characteristics of their white counterparts. Most had prior legislative experience in one or both houses of the state legislature and/or served as delegates to the state or national Republican conventions, and one, Alonzo Ransier of South Carolina, served as lieutenant governor before being elected to Congress in 1872 (Christopher 1976). In the twentieth century, black congressmen also displayed the same political attributes as did their white counterparts. Some had substantial legislative experience as did Augustus Hawkins, who served twenty-eight years in the California assembly before being elected to Congress in 1962. Others, such as Adam Clayton Powell, a popular Harlem minister, held no prior office but were widely known in their districts. Until 1970, successful black congressional candidates came from majority black districts in the North, but followed the same diverse paths to Washington as did white representatives.

Geography was less of a bar to the election of women (a few women were even elected from southern districts in the thirties and forties), but there were other substantial barriers to gaining election to Congress. Conventionally held beliefs regarding sex roles were one. In the early twentieth century many people argued that women's character would be corrupted by the dirtiness connected with politics, and women should remain in the home with their children instead of entering the public arena. In some areas of the country, such as the South, these attitudes were even more strongly held than they were in the nation as a whole. These views held at all levels, so it was difficult for women to gain political experience, an often necessary prerequisite for running for Congress. Some women partially overcame these barriers by following on their husbands' coattails. But, as Gertzog (1984) puts it, most eligible congressional widows were not nominated to succeed their husbands in Congress, so the matrimonial connection is overstated. But, as he details, most of those nominated went on to win election, and several served long and distinguished careers. Once in office, female representatives had the advantage of incumbency in subsequent races, and since many were mature there was no prejudice against them that they should be engaged in child rearing. Nonetheless, the paths of women to Congress prior to 1970 were less conventional than those followed by white or black males. They tended to have less legislative experience and to be older when elected than did men (Kirkpatrick 1974, Diamond 1977).

Some of the attitudinal barriers to the election of women also inhibited them from running for office. It takes a good deal of self-assertiveness to run for any office, and in the past women were told that such behavior was unladylike. Even when a woman was able to overcome this attitude personally, voters might view her unfavorably if they saw her as being too assertive (Mandel 1981). In the past, when a man was elected to

Congress, people expected his wife to be supportive whether she went to Washington or stayed home. A married female candidate had the choice of asking her husband to uproot his career or face questions about her marriage. All candidates in the past might have some self-doubts, but our social construct seemed to force their confrontation with female candidates.

During the 1970s and 1980s, the electoral picture changed for both black and female candidates. Some of the old stereotypes that inhibited these candidates in the past began to break down, voter attitudes began to change, and the numbers of blacks and women elected to Congress increased. It is to these changes in voter and candidate attitudes of the seventies and eighties and their impact on the structure of congressional elections that we turn in chapter 2.

NOTES

1. Margaret Conway (1991) provides a succinct introduction to the definitional problem inherent in the term *representation*.

2. Edmund Burke, the eighteenth-century member of Parliament, stated the view clearly in a speech to his constituents in Bristol (1948, 29–31).

3. The intellectual climate that enabled women to gain the vote in western states in the nineteenth century is detailed in Alan Grimes (1967).

4. The various legal means used to exclude blacks from voting in the South are examined in J. Morgan Kousser (1974).

5. The political gains made by women and the continuing limits that female political leaders faced are detailed in Jeane Kirkpatrick (1974), Leila Rupp and Verta Taylor (1987), and Cynthia Harrison (1988).

6. The Voting Rights Act of 1965 and its 1970, 1975, and 1982 extensions and their impacts are examined in Steven Lawson (1976), Lawson (1985), Howard Ball, Dale Krane, and Thomas Lauth (1982), Armand Derfner (1984), Drew Days and Lani Guinier (1984), Milton Morris (1984), and Harold Stanley (1987).

7. While lobbyists from feminist organizations encouraged female representatives to follow black representatives in forming a caucus, they failed to do so for much of the seventies in part because of the opposition of three senior women in the House—Edith Green, Julia Butler Hansen, and Leonor Sullivan (Hartmann 1989).

8. The inclusion of women in the Civil Rights Act of 1964 came about partially because of political maneuvering by the bill's opponents, who hoped to kill it by including women (Brauer 1983, Hartmann 1989).

Chapter Two

The Representation of Blacks and Women since 1970: An Era of Change

During the seventies the number of female and black elected officials at all levels of government increased steadily. In 1970, there were ten women in the House of Representatives in addition to Margaret Chase Smith in the Senate, and nine black representatives and one senator, Edward Brooke (Kohn 1980, Christopher 1976). By 1980, the number of women in the House had increased to sixteen in addition to Nancy Landon Kassenbaum in the Senate, and the number of blacks had increased to seventeen, all in the House (Kohn 1980, Williams 1982). By early 1990 the numbers stood at twenty-three black Representatives, twenty-six female representatives, and two women in the Senate.[1] During the seventies the number of women in Congress fluctuated, reaching a high of nineteen in the House in the ninety-fourth Congress (1975–1977), a number that had been reached earlier in the eighty-seventh Congress (1961–1963) (Kohn 1980). The number of black representatives grew steadily during the seventies in spite of the defeat of Senator Brooke in 1978. The gains in the number of black elected officials at the state and local levels were even greater than in the House, although in 1980 only 1 percent of all elected officials in the United States were black (Williams 1982). The electoral successes of the seventies paved the way for the candidacies of other women and blacks during the eighties.

Probably the most important considerations governing the election of blacks to Congress in 1970 were the candidate's race and the racial makeup of the district, factors still prevalent today. In 1970, all black representatives were elected from majority black districts, but by 1988, seven black representatives were elected from minority black districts. Nevertheless, the growth in the number of black representatives over the twenty-year period has been heavily dependent on a large black population in the district. By 1988, only two majority black districts were represented by whites: New Jersey's Tenth District, represented by Peter Rodino who retired in 1988 and was replaced by Donald Payne, a black, and Louisiana's Second District, represented by Lindy Boggs.[2] Otherwise, black candidates made inroads in districts in which blacks were not a majority but were at least 30 percent of the population. As John O'Loughlin (1979) suggests, a 30 percent black population in the district seems to be a threshold figure as black participation and the electability of black candidates seems to go up substantially in districts with at least a 30 percent black population. However, two congressmen, Ronald Dellums (CA 8) and Alan Wheat (MO 5), represent districts that have less than 30 percent black populations (Duncan 1989, 116, 860).

Still, most blacks have been elected to represent blacks. The results of the 1990 census and subsequent redrawing of congressional district boundaries could have a profound impact on black representation, particularly in the South where the black population of several congressional districts presently stands at the 30 to 40 percent level.[3] Redrawing district boundaries may lead to the creation of three or more additional black majority districts in the South for the 1992 elections. During the seventies, black congressional candidates had to overcome incumbents and raise the political awareness of the black population without totally alienating the white population. In the eighties, black congressional candidates followed this same path and expanded their reach in districts in which blacks were not a majority. In 1986, the first nonurban black in the twentieth century gained election to Congress when Mike Espey defeated the incumbent Webb Franklin to represent Mississippi's second district. Nonetheless, Espey's rural district, which includes the Delta, has a 58 percent black population (Duncan 1989, 828), indicative of a reasonable chance of success for a black candidate.

Elsewhere in the South, racial gerrymandering and open primaries with runoff elections have been used to dilute black voting strength (Lawson 1985). In one sense the Supreme Court's "one person, one vote" ruling of the sixties was counterproductive for increasing black representation. The ruling gave local officials the incentive to redistrict, which they often did in a fashion so as to dilute black voting strength (Parker 1984). Methods to dilute black voting strength have been divided into four categories by Parker (1984): at-large elections, "cracking," "stacking," and "packing." At-large elections enabled white leaders to limit black participation in local government, but to have no impact on congressional elections. "Cracking" occurs when a district with a large black population is broken up into two or more districts creating black minorities. A notorious example is the Mississippi Third District, which comprised the Delta from 1882 to 1966. The district had a 66 percent black population in 1960. In 1966, the Mississippi legislature divided the district between four of the five Mississippi districts (Parker 1984) guaranteeing that no black candidate could be elected in any of the four new districts. Only in 1984, when the district boundaries were redrawn, was this situation corrected. "Stacking" occurs when a large minority population is combined with a larger white population to dilute minority voting strength—an option often followed with state legislative districts. "Packing" is when a minority voting population is overconcentrated in one district at the 80 percent level or higher. Even though this option may yield one seat to the minority population, it may have been possible for them to have obtained two seats had packing not occurred. Some northern urban districts seem to exhibit the characteristics of being packed so as to concentrate black voting strength. While most of the minority vote dilution has occurred in the South and Southwest, some of the tactics described above have been used elsewhere as well.

Federal courts have gradually whittled away racially gerrymandered districts in the South, and in the eighties have also called into account at-large elections when they seemed to be racially motivated.[4] Interestingly, federal courts have been operating with a 65 percent rule in regard to minority vote dilution. Because of such factors as lower black and Hispanic turnout, the courts have adopted a 65 percent black or Hispanic population as necessary to ensure the election of black or Hispanic candidates, and have looked with disfavor on redistricting schemes that distribute the minority population in such a fashion that the figure is not achieved in an area where it otherwise would be possible to achieve (Parker 1984). Sixty-five percent is substantially higher than O'Loughlin's (1979) 30 percent minimum and seems to belie the electoral success of several of the black congressional delegation. Indeed, some scholars (Brace et al. 1988, 56) go so far as to argue that the "use of the 65 percent figure may have the same effect as the classic gerrymander," as it concentrates black voters in one district to the detriment of black candidates elsewhere.

While most nineteenth-century black congressmen had prior political experience when they were elected to Congress, gaining political experience has always been harder for black politicians than it has been for white politicians. Particularly in the South, the civil rights movement opened up many new options for would-be black politicians. In 1970, there were 92 black county officials and 169 members of state legislatures, by 1980 the numbers had climbed to 451 and 323 respectively (Williams 1982), and by 1985 the numbers stood at 611 and 392 (Williams 1987). These officeholders, in addition to some big-city mayors and council members, became potential congressional candidates in terms of political experience even though most did not run for Congress.

Of course, not all successful congressional candidates have prior political experience. The civil rights movement helped provide a springboard for the election to Congress of Andrew Young in 1972 and John Lewis in 1986, both from Atlanta. As more blacks gain political experience, the bar of prior experience will become even less of a hindrance.

Increasing the number of black representatives during the seventies and eighties has been a two-step process. First, candidates had to convince black voters to register and turn out to vote in majority black districts. Second, black candidates had to worry about alienating white voters to gain election in mixed districts.

Most black congressional candidates during this period have been Democrats, although a few Republican challengers have emerged. While most black voters switched to the Democratic party as a result of the New Deal and remained in the party because of Lyndon Johnson's efforts in behalf of civil rights, the growth of a black middle-class consciousness has led some blacks to switch their party affiliation in the eighties. Nonetheless, running under the Democratic standard has been a prerequisite to election for black congressional candidates since the defeat of Senator Edward Brooke in 1978.[5] Unfortunately for southern black congressional candidates, running as Democrats is no longer a guarantee of election.

Party support has been an important component of most black (and white) candidates' campaigns in the past. Several black Republican congressmen of the nineteenth century were state and national party activists (Christopher 1976). Some twentieth-century black representatives, such as William Dawson of Chicago (Christopher 1976), have been powers in their local party establishments. Party support helped in getting out the vote in addition to providing financial support. As the party system came upon hard times during the seventies, this avenue of support was weakened just at the moment more black candidates were emerging to take advantage of it.

Female congressional candidates face similar barriers including reactionary voter attitudes, lack of prior political experience, and dwindling party support. While fewer women have been elected to Congress from the South than from other regions, geography has been less of a barrier to female candidates than it has been to black candidates. Party affiliation does not seem to play a role in women's political campaigns as women have run successfully on the tickets of both parties.

One examination of voter attitudes toward female candidates, based on data from the early seventies, concludes that women were perceived as having unique qualifications for public office, but qualifications that were related to a perception of women that might actually limit the attractiveness of female candidates for higher political office (Mueller 1986). Mueller concluded that female candidates were seen as nurturing and hence well qualified to deal with issues such as child care or education. While these qualifications might make them attractive candidates for state legislatures, they were less helpful for offices in which a demonstration of mastery, such as the ability to deal with going to war or strengthening the economy, was considered important. Black women candidates were likely to be doubly disadvantaged because blacks were more likely than were whites to argue that "women should take care of running their homes and leave running the country to men" (Darcy and Hadley 1988, 635).

Interestingly, the higher the office held, the more female officeholders described their qualifications in gender-neutral terms (Mueller 1986). It seems successful women congressional candidates were able to portray a balanced picture of nurturance *and* mastery. This assumption lends weight to Diane Fowlkes (1984), who describes a process of countersocialization through which some women developed the political ambition necessary for them to compete for political office. These voter and candidate attitudes affect all aspects of the electoral process for female candidates from recruitment to endorsements and funding to the ultimate voting decisions (Mandel 1981). Other research, however, suggests that after candidate party and incumbency status were taken into account, the sex of the candidate contributed little explanatory power (Darcy and Schramm 1977). In spite of seeming contradictions, it appears that female congressional candidates were somewhat disadvantaged during the seventies, an observation confirmed by the slow rate of increase of female representatives during the decade.

Another aspect of female electability during the seventies came from the debate concerning the Equal Rights Amendment (ERA). If nothing else, the debate over the ERA led many women to become politically active. One issue debated during the drive for ratification was the role of women in society, a debate that often mirrored the attitudes described above. Even though the ERA was not ratified, the debate helped to contribute to an increased acceptance of women's role in the political arena as well as leading more women than before to run for office.

While the struggle for ERA and civil rights raised female political participation to historic levels, congressional challenges evolved more slowly. It appears that by 1980, women were no less ambitious than were men of similar background, but they tended to be older when they first ran for office. Paul Hain (1974) has identified age as an important determinant of political ambition; the older candidates are when they enter politics, the lower their ambition. Because women tend to enter politics at an older age than do men—often after their child-rearing years, he contends that they are less ambitious than male candidates. This contention is especially important when it comes to open-seat races. Such an opportunity must be seized by an ambitious candidate regardless of other aspects of his career.[6] The upshot of these developments has been that since 1974, women have been twice as likely to run as challengers than for open-seat races as open-seat nominations still continue to fall to men (Bernstein 1986). Robert Bernstein contends that women running for open seats encounter men whose ambitions are greater than their own, who work harder to get elected, and who have better credentials than do their female competition.

Bruce Bender (1986) finds age to be an important determinant of a candidate's effort. His explanation is that benefits of being elected to office are reaped over several years, and an older candidate simply has a shorter time horizon to collect. This age impact has a disproportionate impact on women: they, because of their age, are competing for an office with less "value" than that promised their younger (male) opponents.

Whatever the explanation, more women have run as challengers than for open seats. In 1986, female candidates won three of the seven open-seat races they contested, but only one of thirty-six races they entered as challengers. In 1988, one of four female candidates for an open seat won, but only one of thirty-two female challengers won. As is the case for men, when women run as candidates for open seats they have a reasonable chance for success, but their chances as challengers are slim. But, as the 1986 and 1988 results suggest, Fowlkes (1984) may be right in her contention that more-ambitious women are coming forward since women contested seven open seats in 1986 and four open seats in 1988. Part of the problem is that most nonincumbent congressional candidates have to run as challengers.[7]

One account of female electability to the House of Representatives concluded that by the mid-1980s, voter bias against women had a small effect on the electability of women while bias in favor of women had a larger impact (Darcy, Welch, Clarke 1987). Female candidates had seemingly overcome most of the lingering doubt that they were not tough enough to deal with issues requiring a firm hand. This change came about for several reasons. An important one has been the success of female representatives, governors, and mayors. The voters may still see female candidates as nurturing, but they also see them as able to demonstrate mastery when called upon. The change in voter attitudes may have also come from how candidates have presented themselves. Based on 1984's congressional results, Patrick Pierce (1989) maintains that candidates present a different set of gender role characteristics to the voters than they have of themselves. Also important in Pierce's results is the political culture of the district as female candidates partially target their presentation of gender characteristics based on district attitudes. In one sense this is no different than candidates adjusting their stands on the issues to reflect district attitudes.

By the late 1980s, female candidates seemed to have been able to capitalize on both their vulnerability as women and a voter acceptance of them as "tough" candidates. Attacks on female candidates can easily bring charges of sexism, while fewer voters than before seem to give credence to assertions that female candidates are stepping out of an acceptable role. One writer of precepts for male candidates even goes so far as to list ways to attack female and black candidates without suffering charges of sexism or racism (Beiler 1990).[8] The apparent voter acceptance of tough stances by female candidates has proceeded apace with a growth of female political ambition in the 1980s. The vice-presidential candidacy of Geraldine Ferraro in 1984 helped to foster both a view among women that they could run for any office and a voter approval of their candidacies. Particularly among black women the experience of the civil rights movement has been important in leading them to seek and gain political office (Darcy and Hadley 1988), even if few have been elected to Congress as yet. The attitudinal shift among would-be candidates and voters has worked to the advantage of female candidates in the eighties, an advantage that at least some political consultants consider to be significant when a woman is running against a male candidate.

Party ties have been an important resource for many candidates in the past, but women generally have remained outside party councils. Male party activists could often count on party support when they announced for office, but female activists often found their candidacies discouraged outright or found that they were shunted off into lesser races (Carroll 1985). In 1978, for example, when Marge Roukema announced her candidacy for a congressional seat in New Jersey, party leaders urged her to run for a county-level office instead. Only after she won the primary with her own organization did the Republican party provide any support (Mandel 1981, 103). In many ways winning the nomination proved to be the hard part for female congressional candidates in the 1960s and 1970s.[9] Even when a party organization encouraged women to run for Congress, it was often because the race was hopeless. Party leaders could say they were supportive of female candidates when in fact they supported them only as sacrificial lambs running against entrenched incumbents. Ironically, as women became more established as candidates during the seventies, the parties' impact as providers of election services was waning. During the eighties both female and male candidates relied on their own organizations to provide many of the services, such as fund raising and get-out-the-vote drives, that parties had provided in the past. While Paul Herrnson (1988) may be correct in maintaining that parties are reviving, it remains to be seen how helpful this revival will be to female or black candidates.

An important resource provided by political parties for congressional candidates in the past, one essential to victory, is financial support. Here too, female candidates have been at a disadvantage in the past, a disadvantage that persisted into the 1980s. The standard argument suggests women have been less socialized to ask for money for their campaigns than have male candidates, and they have not been integrated into social or occupational networks that would give them access to large sums of campaign money (Carroll 1985, Mandel 1981). In the past this was true, although some women were able to draw upon their husbands for campaign support. Changes in campaign finance laws in the early seventies diminished the impact of big contributors in congressional races. Barbara Burrell (1985) analyzed campaign financing from 1972 to 1982 and found a curvilinear relationship with the levels of women's congressional campaign funds closer to that of their male counterparts in 1972 and 1982 than in the years in between. Neither Burrell (1985) nor Carol Uhlaner and Kay Schlozman (1986), using data for the 1980 election, found any difference between the funding of comparable female and male candidates. Their results seem to conflict with those reported by Carroll (1985) and Mandel (1981). Carroll and Mandel, however, rely on anecdotal evidence while Burrell and Uhlaner and Schlozman pursue rigorous statistical models. Some of the opposition to fund-raising reported by Carroll could also be found among male candidates (Adamany and Agree 1975), as almost no candidates are comfortable asking for money. Once the impact of big contributors was washed out, fund-raising had to be done in a different fashion, one in which the candidate's gender seems to be less important than in the past. Nonetheless, the implicit question remains: does residual opposition to women as political candidates affect their ability to raise money?

While political action committees have become major sources of funds for many candidates, some also provide other services such as polling or organizational assistance, and a few even help to recruit candidates. Here too, women and blacks were at a disadvantage in the seventies as they were often "out of the loop," although this began to change by the early eighties (Wilhite and Theilmann 1986). More recently the National Organization of Women and its political action committee (NOWPAC) have actively supported women's candidacies and encouraged women to run for Congress, altering the old slogan "a woman's place is in the house," by adding "and in the Senate." Some women's PACs even went as far as to address the financial disadvantages of challengers by contributing almost exclusively to them (Kleeman 1983). Representative John Conyers organized the Parker-Coltrane PAC to support black candidates (Sabato 1984), but with its modest resources it has been less effective in fostering the growth in the number of black congressional candidates.

Changes regarding black and female political participation hinted at in 1970 had become reality by the end of the eighties. Writing at the end of the sixties, Sidney Verba and Norman Nie (1972) found stark differences in the participation rates of blacks and whites, differences that were at least partially attributable to race. Although whites continued to be more active politically than were blacks at the end of the eighties, the differences were largely the result of class, not race (Secret and Welch 1989). The increased political activity of a group is no guarantee that one of its members will run for office or be elected, but it enhances the probability. The increase in the number of black elected officials has widened the potential candidate pool, further enhancing the chances of successful black candidates. But, in spite of notable successes in several cities and the election of Douglas Wilder as first lieutenant governor and then governor of Virginia in 1989, blacks still were not being elected to Congress in large numbers by the end of the eighties. The incumbency bias is part of the answer, but a question of implicit, if not explicit, structural barriers to the election of blacks remains unanswered.

It is possible for blacks to win statewide races as was demonstrated by Douglas Wilder. Conversely, Tom Bradley, the mayor of Los Angeles, lost a bid to become governor of California in 1986, a loss that has been partially attributed to race (Sonenshein 1990). In his analysis of the lessons from the statewide races of Edward Brooke, Tom Bradley, and Douglas Wilder, Raphael Sonenshein (1990) concludes that black candidates can win such races but they must be able to benefit from populations with liberal racial attitudes, a positive political situation, and the ability to employ a flexible campaign strategy that enables them to turn out black voters without alienating white voters. While black candidates have been able to win congressional seats in situations in which these three criteria have not been fulfilled, those districts usually have a large black population. As black candidates vie for seats in minority black districts, the ability to turn out black voters without also turning out antiblack voters becomes increasingly important.

Although differences in the participation rates of women and men were less than those for blacks and whites in 1970, women's participation rates changed enough during the seventies that residual differences can be attributed to class, not gender (Poole and Zeigler 1985, Secret and Welch 1989). Even when older women were less politically active than their male contemporaries, their daughters were as politically active as their sons. Structural barriers to the election of women seemed to be breaking down in earnest during the seventies and eighties. Yet the number of women in Congress remained fairly constant during the eighties. How can these trends be reconciled?

A remaining barrier to increased representation of women and blacks in Congress is incumbency. Throughout the eighties, incumbent representatives have been reelected at a rate well over 90 percent, reaching a high of 98 percent in 1988. The strengths of incumbents have long been recognized; Richard Fenno (1978) pointed out that we hate Congress but love our representatives. The strengths of incumbents are well detailed (e.g., Goldenberg and Traugott 1984, Jacobson 1987, Salmore and Salmore 1989), and include name recognition, paid campaigning time, postal franking, skill in campaigning acquired through practice, and access to campaign funds as well as large war chests. This barrier may be altered a bit in 1992 as a result of redistricting, although incumbents will call in their favors in state legislatures to secure "safe" districts. In chapter 3 we will examine the impact of money on overcoming the hurdle of incumbency.

During the 1980s, many of the previous structural barriers to the election of women to Congress broke down. Voters accepted female candidates for whom they were—candidates for Congress—rather than women out of place in society. To be sure, not everyone's attitudes changed in the same way. As Pierce (1989) points out in regard to the 1984 elections, the political culture of a district affected how a female candidate presented herself to the electorate even though candidates handled the question of gender in a variety of ways. Women had also gained increased political experience, leading to a larger number of creditable candidates than ever before. Moreover, political slatemakers did not turn to women as simply sacrificial lambs, as had been done in the past. The increase in the number of candidates—sixty-two women ran for Congress in 1986 and fifty-nine in 1988—also should help additional women decide to run for Congress. Role models for prospective candidates abounded by the end of the decade. During the 1980s there seemed to be little unanimity among female congressional candidates. Some were liberal and others conservative, just as were the female voters of their districts. In sum, there is no block women's vote for female candidates. Conversely, there is no block anti-female vote. An increase in the cost of getting elected during the decade raises the question of funding once again. Even if voters no longer discriminate against women, do funding sources discriminate against them, hampering their chances of election?

Black congressional hopefuls have made less progress than have their female counterparts during the 1980s. Racism may be on the decline in American society, but the number of black representatives is changing at a snail's pace. A major barrier for black would-be members of Congress appears to be the percentage of black voters in the district. While there are signs that this barrier is weakening, there still seems to be a residuum of black bloc voting as successful black candidates have run on the Democratic slate, and few black Republican congressional candidates have surfaced. There also appears to be a reservoir of antiblack voting among some voters. In spite of advances, far fewer blacks run for Congress than do women. This may stem from a lack of desire or self-selection. Do prospective black candidates consider the odds and remain where they are? Even so, there are several black mayors and even some statewide officials. One obstacle that any potential candidate must consider is raising money. Does a discrepancy in funding continue to bar black candidates particularly when the possibility of increasingly expensive elections looms and as black challengers must contest elections in competitive and majority-white districts? These obstacles are formidable, but blacks must run in majority white districts if they are to increase their numbers in Congress. Elections in white majority districts are likely to require significant amounts of money for black candidates to be successful.

Many of the barriers to the election of blacks and women to Congress have been overcome during the seventies and eighties. Voters have become more favorably inclined to female candidates, although there remains a residual antiblack bias working against some black congressional candidates. The racial makeup of a district is still a factor in the election of black candidates, although this barrier, too, has been breached. Women and blacks are more willing to run for office now than they were in the past, and many have done so successfully at municipal, county, and state levels, deepening the eligible pool for congressional seats. Both political parties encourage qualified blacks and women to run for Congress, and the parties support them in competitive situations. Incumbency remains a major obstacle to increasing the number of women and blacks in Congress. Incumbents can be beaten, open seats are available, and black and female incumbents must be reelected. Chapter 3 will examine one factor that touches incumbents, challengers, and open-seat candidates: electoral resources, specifically money.

NOTES

1. Twenty-five women won election to Congress in 1988. Jill Long, who lost in November 1988, won a special election in 1989 to succeed Daniel Coats in the Indiana Fourth District when Coats was appointed to Dan Quayle's Senate seat. Twenty-nine women were elected to the House in November 1990.

2. Lindy Boggs retired from the House in 1990 and was succeeded by a black, William Jefferson.

3. Focusing on black and Hispanic districts, Kimball Brace et al. (1988) conclude that a black plurality and a combined black and Hispanic population above 50 percent ensures that a district will eventually have a black representative.

4. Joe Darden (1984) argues that in instances where the black population is large enough, black representation on city councils is improved by the use of at-large rather than district elections.

5. In November 1990, the voters in the Connecticut Fifth District elected the first black Republican representative since the 1930s, sending Gary Franks to Congress to succeed John Rowland, who ran for governor.

6. Some candidates who originally bypassed a chance to run for an open seat were later able to unseat the incumbent. For example, Louise Slaughter preferred to remain in the New York state legislature in 1984 rather than run for the Thirtieth District seat that came open when Barber Conable retired. Slaughter strengthened her image in the statehouse, acquired some IOUs, and was able to take advantage of Fred Eckert's neglect of the constituency to capture the House seat in 1986 (Fowler and McClure 1989).

7. The difficulty entailed for women in increasing their numbers by running as challengers has led Robert Darcy and James Choike (1986) to suggest that women should place more attention on retaining incumbents in the House instead of gaining new seats as a means of increasing the number of women in Congress.

8. Beiler's advice brought hostile letters, an apology from the editor of *Campaigns & Elections*, and a column by Sharon Rodine (1990), the president of the National Women's Political Caucus, advising female candidates how to counter such tactics.

9. This point is supported by Robert Bernstein (1986), who argues that women receive a larger percentage of challenger nominations than they do open-seat slots, leading them to run in races in which they normally have scant expectation of victory.

Chapter Three

Campaign Contributions: A Historic Overview

Campaigning for public office in the United States is costly as candidates want to gain name recognition, publicize stands on the issues, and acquire and motivate supporters. Even in the colonial era, candidates were expected to stand drinks for the crowd. None of this can be accomplished without financial resources. Until the ratification of the Seventeenth Amendment in 1913, candidates for the Senate primarily directed their attention to state legislatures rather than to voters, but House candidates have always had to present a more broad-based appeal.

Today, candidates for House and Senate seats face an increasingly expensive process in gaining office. Senate campaigns cost more than do House elections, with the average figures being $2,802,000 and $274,000 respectively.[1] Open-seat races are usually more expensive than others, for example, spending (expressed in constant 1988 dollars) by incumbents and candidates for open seats increased 60 percent during the 1980s, while challengers' spending actually dropped by 17 percent (in real terms) over the same period (Magleby and Nelson 1990). Challenger funding stood at 61 percent of incumbent funding in 1980, but was only 31 percent of incumbent funding in 1988. The magnitude of the disparity in contributions is even greater because challengers and open-seat candidates tend to spend every dollar they raise while incumbents often spend a fraction of what they receive, letting their growing war chests deter future challengers. Open-seat candidates have generally been able to raise large sums, but these expensive contests usually absorb every nickel. The dregs are left to the poor challenger who has a great need to raise money—taking on an entrenched incumbent is costly—but who finds it difficult to do so.

Much of this campaign money is consumed by media expenses: newpaper advertising, billboards and yard signs, and bumper stickers and other paraphernalia, radio, and especially television time. Other expenses include telephone and postage costs, office and equipment rental, travel expenses, and salaries.[2] Broadcast expenses alone accounted for 15.8 percent of the expenses of House candidates in the 1985–86 election cycle (Magleby and Nelson 1990), and such expenses can go much higher, especially for challengers. Many candidates are also turning to consultants for advice in all stages of their campaigns. Consultants may be able to increase candidates' war chests, but their services are not cheap. Most races do not utilize every avenue of approaching voters; some candidates in urban races involving a few city blocks eschew television as not being cost-effective. Some districts are in several overlapping television markets (such as New Jersey districts or some rural districts bordered by several markets), and these candidates often rule out television. Conversely, television time is inexpensive in some markets, and candidates there buy large amounts of time. Some races are still won on a shoestring. In 1988, Sidney Yates (IL 9) won re-election with 66 percent of the vote while spending $122,900, a fraction of typical incumbent spending. Candidates are aware of the increasing costs of campaigning, and a significant expense is that of fund-raising. Fund-raising costs take many forms, dollars naturally, but also the time that could be used in meeting the voters, and in loss of self-esteem. Most candidates would still echo Hubert Humphrey's lament: "Searching for campaign money is a disgusting, degrading, demeaning experience (Adamany and Agree 1975, 8)." However, some candidates seem to enjoy raising money and often are able to raise large sums because of their willingness to hustle.

MONEY AND CAMPAIGNS IN THE PAST

Prior to the Civil War, congressional campaign expenditures were much lower and generally involved expenditures by the political parties. In order to present a broad-based front on the issues, national party organizations might support newspapers such as Philip Freneau's *National Gazette*, which the Democratic-Republican party subsidized in 1791. Congressional candidates usually did not campaign in the modern sense, preferring to woo the voters based on their merits, a few rounds of drinks on election day, and a reliance on the party to turn out the voters. The rise of the spoils system, dating from the 1820s, began to change this approach. As elected officials began to reward their supporters with political jobs, they began to expect financial support in return. Richard Jensen estimates that in the first half of the nineteenth century one patronage position existed for every 100 voters, public employees that were expected to devote time to the cause, so that "American politics in the nineteenth century was publicly financed in effect, though not by law (1983, 31)."

The expansion of the electorate also played a role, as getting out the vote often meant buying the vote. In 1832, for example, the price of an uncommitted vote in New York City was reputed to be five dollars (Thayer 1973, 29). Nonetheless, the impact of money seems to have been felt (in different ways) more in presidential and state and local races than in congressional elections. This situation reflected both the demand and the supply of funds. Congressional candidates generally spent modestly and so needed little, and contributors preferred to allocate their money to races that promised to be more directly productive for their needs, such as for city councils that controlled public works contracts.

Following the Civil War the situation changed. The flow of money into political campaigns (and elected officials' pockets) became a torrent at all levels. In part the role of money increased in response to increasing costs of election. A larger, more-diverse electorate increased the costs of campaigning. Another aspect of elections was also becoming more expensive—the actual cost of obtaining votes. The reign of Boss Tweed in New York in the 1860s was only too symptomatic of the general level of corruption in the political world. Buying votes became common, as did the selling of influence by politicians. During the last quarter of the nineteenth century the alliance of business and politics became solidified as corporate money openly flowed into party coffers and candidates' pockets. Political party organizations continued to play a major role in fund-raising from corporations and individuals and in doling out these receipts to candidates. Party loyalty continued to be a prerequisite for congressional candidates to obtain party funds and votes. Congressional elections produced fewer of the costly factional battles that enlivened some Senate races, so costs remained moderate throughout the nineteenth century.

Senatorial elections were particularly open to bribery—a few well-placed contributions in the state legislature could ensure the outcome. Some money men, such as Collis Huntington in California, who with his associates already "owned" the state legislature, could easily obtain election to the Senate. Others had to buy their way in. In 1896, when he decided to be elected to the Senate, Boies Penrose, the Pennsylvania boss, was forced to spend half a million dollars in order to bribe the 254 members of the Pennsylvania legislature. His opponent, John Wanamaker, mistakenly thought $400,000 would be enough to gain the seat (Thayer 1973, 47). Penrose in turn tapped the pockets of steel men such as Andrew Carnegie, Henry Clay Frick, and Charles Schwab. The industrialists expected Penrose and his fellow Senators to safeguard their interests in return for their contributions.[3]

Industrialists were not alone in entering into a quid pro quo relationship with politicians in the latter half of the nineteenth century. Public employees helped to fill the governing party's war chest on pain of losing their jobs. In Pennsylvania in 1882 every public employee received the following message:

> Two percent of your salary is _____. Please remit promptly. At the close of the campaign we shall place a list of those who have not paid in the hands of the head of the department you are in. (Thayer 1973, 38)

Tactics such as this enabled political parties to support favored candidates while punishing backsliders. They controlled who ran for office by funding favored candidates, leaving others to fend for themselves.

Even though some candidates might be able to finance their elections with their own and friends' resources, many had to turn to the parties for assistance in funding and acquiring votes. Nineteenth-century political parties were more than sources of campaign money—they usually controlled the nomination process, ran the campaign, and mobilized the voters. Party organizations themselves were often directed by leaders such as Penrose or Tweed, and, as it continued unabated, boss rule led to complaints by political opponents and the friends of good government. In any case, boss rule helped to drive up the cost of election through an emphasis on increasing the take from various sources.

Political fund-raising came of age in the presidential campaign of 1896. The McKinley campaign exhibited many political firsts such as its skilled merchandising of the candidate and the use of technology, the telephone. Most notably it contributed the first modern fund-raiser: Mark Hanna. Hanna had long been involved in Ohio politics and had supported the political ascent of McKinley in the state. In 1896 he personally bore most of the presidential nomination costs of McKinley, a sum well over $100,000 (Thayer 1973, 48–49). After McKinley garnered the nomination, Hanna came into his own as he levied a tariff on corporations and banks. If a contribution was too low, he returned it with a pointed note to reconsider, and if too much was sent, the donor received a refund. A man of scrupulous personal honesty, Hanna kept meticulous records as well as refusing to make promises in return for contributions or to spend money buying votes. Such behavior shocked the political bosses of the time, but it produced results. Herbert Alexander (1984) estimates the McKinley campaign spent $3.35 million, but other estimates are much higher. Hanna's tactics worked at the presidential level, but at other levels it continued to be business as usual. Hanna became a prototype for future fund-raisers, but most candidates relied on tried-and-true methods, which included fat cats, passing the hat at rallies, and other small-scale, time-intensive forms of raising money.

The role of money during campaigns and afterward did not go unnoticed by reformers. Newspaper stories and the biting cartoons of Thomas Nast contributed to the downfall of the Tweed ring in New York in 1871. Tweed and his Tammany associates were more concerned with lining their own pockets than with simply winning elections. For them, winning elections was a means to an end, and their deeds did not directly increase the costs of election. Yet machine politics made for more-costly elections as the machines demanded money from many sources and provided largesse to their followers through jobs, cash, and even donations of food and clothing. The type of corruption engaged in by the Tweed ring continued to be condemned and just as often ignored well into the twentieth century.

The spoils system came under fire almost from its inception. By the late 1870s, civil service reform associations had formed in thirteen states. The assassination of President Garfield by a frustrated office seeker in 1881 served as the catalyst for reform, and two years later Congress passed the Civil Service Act. It provided that certain classes of federal employees would be hired and promoted on merit rather than on political affiliation. Although at first only 10 percent of federal employees were covered by the legislation, later presidents added more employees by excutive order. New York and Massachusetts followed suit in 1883 and 1884, but other states and most local governments were slow to adopt merit systems. In one sense these reforms had little impact on congressional elections because senators and representatives controlled few patronage jobs. However, civil service reform at the state and local levels diminished the flow of money into the coffers of party organizations, money that some senators and representatives controlled as party bosses or had allocated to them by the party. In some cities, such as Chicago, patronage continued to be the order of the day, allowing the party in power ready access to campaign funds.

Party money continued to be a major source of funds for political campaigns in the late nineteenth century and well into the twentieth century. As the McKinley campaign demonstrates, corporations were another source. Individuals also made their mark. The financier August Belmont contributed $200,000 to the Democratic presidential campaign of Alton Parker in 1904. This was, however, an era of reform expressed in first Populism and then Progressivism. The Progressives, in particular, were anxious to "clean up" government by weakening the impact of money in elections. In their desire for clean government the Progressives were forced to launch a challenge against party government, as some Progressives saw government dominated by party organizations as hopelessly corrupt.

Progressives in state legislatures and Congress sponsored legislation designed to limit the influence of what they considered to be harmful influences on the political process. Arising from this impetus and outrage at the large sums of corporate money spent in the elections of 1900 and 1904, Perry Belmont (younger brother of the Democratic money man August Belmont) organized the National Publicity Bill Organization to push for financial disclosure legislation. Representative Samuel McCall (R-MA) introduced a NPBO bill in early 1906 providing for the public disclosure of expenditures and receipts of any committee active in national elections in two or more states. Congressional district and state committees were omitted for fear of southern antagonism (Mutch 1988, 8). The bill came to naught, partially because of fears that it was a partisan measure designed to protect Democratic committees such as Tammany Hall. When the campaign for the bill began in 1904, Perry Belmont was acting chair of the New York State Democratic committee, giving further ammunition to those who considered the NPBO a Democratic front. The issue did not die, and after much debate Congress passed, and President Taft signed, a financial disclosure bill in 1910. The next year the Democratic-controlled Congress passed further amendments that provided for primary, convention, and preelection statements. More important, Senator James A. Reed (D-MO) introduced a successful amendment that placed a spending limit of $10,000 on campaign spending (Mutch 1988, 12–16). Earlier, with the Tillman Act of 1907, Congress prohibited corporate contributions to national candidates partially in response to allegations of corporate money flowing to the Roosevelt campaign in a quid pro quo arrangement.

Three major issues are evident in these Progressive era reforms. The Progressives maintained: (1) elections cost too much, (2) fund-raising needed to be carried out in the open, and (3) corporate money was bad because corporate leaders expected influence in return for their contributions. These were not purely partisan issues; there were Democrats and Republicans on both sides of all three issues. While spending limits probably disadvantaged Republican candidates, publicity probably hurt Democratic organizations such as Tammany Hall. Although the Republicans benefited more than Democrats did from corporate support, especially in the McKinley-Bryan presidential campaign of 1896, both parties had supporters in the business community. All of these issues have been at the heart of subsequent reform legislation up through the present. None of the reforms directly touched how candidates were chosen, nor did they deal with House campaigns. Even though the reformers might have been concerned with House races, they ignored them for fear of a southern states'-rights backlash and because the big money they considered harmful was flowing to presidential and senatorial campaigns.

Ratification of the Seventeenth Amendment, in 1913, gave election of senators to the people instead of to state legislatures, and this changed their funding picture. Limits on senatorial campaign spending did not survive for long. The Reed amendment had provided for a $10,000 limit or a state-imposed limit, whichever was less, for senatorial campaigns. Michigan mandated a primary spending ceiling of 25 percent of the annual salary ($1,875 for senators) of the office sought. Even for 1918 this was not much money, especially for a statewide race. Truman Newberry's campaign committee spent nearly $180,000 as he pursued the Republican senatorial nomination in 1918, a sum largely contributed by family members. Newberry, an unknown, decided he needed to spend large sums on newspaper advertising and mailings to achieve name recognition because his opponent was Henry Ford. Although spending much less, Ford too exceeded the $1,875 limit, but because his spending was not channeled through a campaign committee the amount is unknown.

In 1919, a federal grand jury indicted Newberry, his committee, and his supporters for violation of the 1911 spending limitations (Mutch 1988, 16–22). Convicted, Newberry was sentenced to a two-year prison term and fined $10,000, while sixteen others were also convicted. The defendants appealed to the Supreme Court and hired the well-respected Charles Evans Hughes as their attorney. In 1921 Hughes argued against the conviction on two grounds: (1) the campaign committee, not Newberry, spent the money, and the committee was not covered by the law, and (2) primaries were not elections within the meaning of the Constitution, so the law did not apply. In its five-to-four decision (*Newberry* v. *U.S.* [256 U.S. 232]) the Supreme Court overturned Newberry's conviction, stating that Congress had overstepped its authority by bringing primaries under federal election law. Not until twenty years later in *U.S.* v. *Classic* (313 U.S. 299) did the Court reject this narrow interpretation in another case relating to federal-state powers.

Even though the role of corporate money had been curtailed by the Tillman Act, large sums continued to flow into campaigns in various ways to supply candidates' and parties' demand. Although most congressional and senatorial candidates no longer bought votes, "treating" continued to be common.

Expenditures for cigars appear in the expense account of candidates in the Pennsylvania Republican Senatorial primary of 1926. Candidates in Massachusetts frequently return [sic] expenditures for "cigars and tobacco." In the 1930 senatorial campaign the Eben Draper Political Committee spent over $500 for this purpose. (Overacker 1932, 35)

In the thirties congressional candidates needed more money in order to take advantage of new developments such as radio. The Democratic National Committee spent $550,000 on radio for Al Smith's presidential campaign in 1928 (Overacker 1932, 28), and congressional campaigns soon began to follow the national model. Moreover, the increasing size of the electorate made reaching voters a more expensive process. Even old-fashioned campaigns, such as Eugene Talmadge's failed Georgia senatorial bid in 1936, were changing as they required increased sums for radio in addition to those for barbeque and transportation. Congressional campaigns continued to be cheaper than senate races (Overacker 1932, 60), but even the costs of running for the House were mounting.

Partially in response to the Teapot Dome scandal, Congress tried again to regulate spending in congressional elections with the Corrupt Practices Act of 1925. It set spending limits of $5,000 for House races and $25,000 for Senate races, while requiring periodic statements listing contributions and expenditures, but the act provided no enforcement mechanism for disclosure. Trying to examine congressional campaign spending records in the late 1920s, Louise Overacker found that:

When one asks for [old reports] one is taken into a tiny wash room where a series of dusty, paper-covered bundles repose upon an upper shelf. By climbing upon a chair and digging about among the bundles one usually finds what one wants if one persists in this "trial and error" method long enough, but there is no file and no system, and for some of the earlier campaigns no record of what is supposed to be there and what is not. When the strings are removed from the brown-paper parcels one is likely to find the oldest of these reports in a very mutilated condition. (1932, 295)

Even when records were present, they were often inaccurate or incomplete. Political committees seeking to influence elections in two or more states also had to file disclosure statements, but few did. Once again, contributions from corporations and national banks were banned, but these prohibitions continued to be skirted with alacrity. The law had so many loopholes as to be nearly unenforceable. No audits were required, and money expended without the candidate's "knowledge and consent" did not fall under the spending limitations. Primary expenditures were exempt, based on the *Newberry* decision. Even the prohibition on corporate contributions could be evaded if corporate officers made contributions individually instead of having the money come directly from the corporation's treasury.

The weakness of the law is evident from a Senate investigation of the Pennsylvania senatorial contest of 1926. Two Republican factions spent $785,000 and $1.8 million respectively in the primary while the Democratic candidate spent $10,000. Various corporate factions backed both Republicans handsomely (three members of the Mellon family alone contributed $173,000), and election day spending was so lavish it took three days to pay off the workers. The Senate Committee on Privileges and Elections refused to seat the Republican winner but also denied the seat to his Democratic opponent. Finally, Governor Gifford Pinochot appointed the Republican loser to the seat, a step unopposed by the Senate (Thayer 1973, 63–64). Not all campaigns were this costly or as corrupt, but it was obvious that few effective limits on campaign spending or contributions existed.

Congress tried to come to grips with the election-funding tangle again in 1939 and 1940 with the passage of the Hatch acts. Taken together, they prohibited political activity, including contributing money to candidates, by all federal employees (and any state employees paid wholly or in part with federal funds), not just those under the civil service system. Subsequently, many postmasters' wives became politically active as a way of circumventing the law. The Hatch Act imposed a $3 million per campaign ceiling on spending by national party committees as well as placing a $5,000 limit on individual contributions to federal candidates. Individuals could, however, contribute to multiple committees working for the same candidate, so the contribution limit was constrainted only by the ability of campaign workers to devise additional committee names. Multiple campaign committees also provided a way for evading the $3 million ceiling since the limit was interpreted as applying to one committee.

Although there continued to be talk of reform in the period immediately after World War II, Congress took no concrete actions for several years. Campaigns were becoming more expensive in the postwar era. Republicans generally enjoyed a financial advantage over Democratic candidates during the fifties in spite of labor political action committee (PAC) contributions that flowed almost exclusively to Democrats (Heard 1960). The Eisenhower presidential campaign of 1952 was the first major television campaign, introducing additional costs to campaigning. Congressional candidates were slow to follow the path of presidential candidates, but during the 1960s television gradually began to come into use in congressional races. Also during the sixties Congress launched two abortive efforts at reform. The Ashmore-Goodell Bill, passed by the Senate in 1966, called for the creation of a bipartisan Federal Election Commission to act as a watchdog over federal campaigns. The never-implemented Long Act of 1966 called for federal subsidies to political parties in presidential elections as a means of curtailing special-interest money. Both pieces of legislation were flawed, yet they indicated a budding reform sentiment in Congress.

Writing in the late 1950s, Alexander Heard found six major characteristics of American campaign finance (Heard 1960, summarized in Sorauf 1988, 21–24). First, large contributors tended to dominate the process. In 1952, for example, around two-thirds of the financing for the presidential election came in sums of $500 and over and more than 85 percent in sums over $100 (Heard 1960, 49). Corrected for inflation, these amounts are $2,065 and $413 in 1986 dollars. During the sixties, "fat cats" continued to be major sources for many candidates at all levels.

Second, the patronage system was still alive and functioning as a funding source during the 1950s. Patronage employees continued to fund local political machines in many areas of the country during the decade, but during the sixties these amounts diminished drastically as many machines received death blows at the hands of the voters, or legislation and court decisions severely restrained their ability to extract contribuions.

Third, congruent with an important role for individual contributors was a limited role for group efforts. Prohibited by law from contributing to political campaigns, corporations channeled their political largesse through their executives. In the fifties the Justice Department brought several legal challenges against labor PACs, largely to no avail (Mutch 1988, 158–65). After surviving the legal challenges of the fifties, labor PACs increased their clout in the sixties, but except for a few scattered races they did not match the overall effort of individual contributors.

Fourth, parties maintained a major position in the funding arena during the fifties, especially the Republican party. During the decade of the sixties the Republicans widened the financial gap between them and the Democrats. In any case both parties were still major players in the funding game at the end of the sixties, although their role was beginning to be challenged.

Fifth, solicitation of funds at the personal level remained the dominant means of fund-raising throughout the period. This point is related to the dominance of "fat cats" who had to be cultivated by well-connected party fund-raisers.

Finally, Heard found that regulation had scant impact on campaign financing. In spite of existing legislation, campaign financing was bound only by the ingenuity of fund-raisers and the potential threat of adverse publicity if discovered.

Pre-1970s campaign financing reform can be characterized as a movement that concentrated largely on presidential and senatorial elections at the national level. The reformers' efforts at limiting campaign receipts and publicizing both receipts and spending were largely ineffectual. Some states also made efforts at campaign finance reform, and by 1960, four states had passed limits on individual contributions, thirty-one states limited campaign expenditures (generally the limits applied to spending carried out at the candidate's direction), and forty-three states had some sort of reporting mechanism for campaign finances (Heard 1960, 344–57; Sorauf 1988, 31–32). The issue of regulating House races often fell into the limbo between Senate elections and purely state races. They were often covered by reform legislation, but as an afterthought. Throughout the period House elections generally cost much less than Senate races. There also seemed to be less of an advantage to being an incumbent representative than being an incumbent senator, as representatives were often agents of a powerful machine, enjoying little autonomy.

CAMPAIGN MONEY IN THE FECA ERA

In spite of their failures the Ashmore-Goodell Bill and the Long Act served to break the ground for the passage of the Federal Election Campaign Act (FECA) of 1971 (passed in January 1972).[4] A comprehensive attempt at reform that replaced earlier campaign finance laws, the FECA:

1. Set limits on media expenditures for candidates for federal elections. These limits were replaced in the 1974 amendments with limits on total spending (partially declared unconstitutional in 1976 in *Buckley* v. *Valeo*, 424 U.S. 1 [1976]).

2. Set a maximum on the amount of money candidates or their immediate families could contribute to their campaigns. This provision was later declared unconstitutional in the *Buckley* decision, although a $50,000 ceiling was imposed for presidential candidates who accept public funding.

3. Provided for officials to oversee reporting for presidential, Senate, and House races. The 1974 amendments centralized this oversight in the Federal Election Commission.

4. Required House and Senate candidates to file duplicate copies of their reports with the secretary of state or other comparable state official in the state in which they were running.

5. Required candidates and political committees to report names, addresses, and business affiliations of all contributors whose aggregate contributions exceeded $100 per calendar year. Also, people who received more than $100 per year from the campaign fund for any services or reimbursements were to be listed. In both cases the amount was raised to $200 by the 1979 amendments.

6. Set reporting deadlines for reporting receipts and expenditures.

7. Required full financial statements from presidential nominating conventions sixty days after the convention. The Revenue Act of 1971 supplemented these regulations by providing for income tax deductions or credits for contributions at all levels. It also instituted the presidential campaign fund income tax checkoff. This latter point was the first successful implementation of reformers' desire for public funding of campaigns.

The financial abuses coming out of the Watergate episode spurred calls for additional campaign finance reform. After acrimonious debate, Congress passed amendments to the FECA that President Ford signed in October 1974. These amendments set up the Federal Election Commission (FEC), whose early tenure was stormy. The legislation also placed limits on candidate contributions to their own campaigns (struck down in *Buckley* v. *Valeo*), on individual contributions ($1,000 per candidate per campaign, with a $25,000 maximum), and on political action committees ($5,000 per candidate per campaign with no aggregate limit).

The last provision has fostered the growth of political action committees (PACs). During the 1940s, labor unions had organized PACs as a means of circumventing legislation designed to thwart their political involvement. The Smith-Connally Act of 1943 brought union treasury funds under the same prohibitions that had long governed corporations. The Congress of Industrial Organizations (CIO) quickly responded by creating a political action committee that used member contributions instead of union treasury funds as a means of circumventing the Smith-Connally Act. The 1907 legislation, which the Smith-Connally Act supplemented, also prohibited direct contributions to federal campaigns. CIO attorneys interpreted the law as restricting contributions but not expenditures on behalf of a candidate (Mutch 1988, 154–55). Even though the Justice Department challenged labor PACs in the courts on several occasions, the courts upheld their legality (Mutch 1988, 156–65). Business had long preferred to have executives make contributions on their behalf, so most corporations were initially uninterested in forming PACs. With the new limits on individual contributions the executive route was closed and political action committees provided businesses an outlet for their political involvement. Other groups, such as trade and membership organizations, like the American Medical Association and the National Rifle Association, followed labor's example in the fifties and sixties. Eventually PACs were organized whose sole reason for being was to influence electoral politics, the nonconnected PACs, such as the National Conservative Political Action Committee, or candidate-centered PACs designed to further the political career of one individual.

Some provisions of the FECA and the 1974 amendments were soon challenged in the courts. The *Buckley* decision struck down the limits candidates could spend on their own campaigns while other cases challenged the very existence of the FEC. The Supreme Court eventually upheld the disclosure provisions of the law and the existence of the FEC, although the FEC had to become a solely executive agency instead of one whose members were nominated by the president and Congress. In 1976 Congress dealt with these Supreme Court decisions by reconstituting the FEC as a bipartisan executive agency and imposing a $50,000 personal contribution limit on presidential candidates who accepted federal matching funds, but imposing no limits on the amount congressional candidates could contribute to their own campaigns.

The FECA continued to be evaluated, and in 1979 Congress passed additional amendments. The thrust of the 1979 amendments was to simplify record-keeping and public-reporting requirments. For example, candidates who received or spent less than $5,000 were exempt from filing disclosure reports, and the threshold limit for reporting itemized contributions was raised from $100 to $200. These amendments also expanded the permissiable role of state and local party committees by allowing them to spend unlimited amounts on certain voter registration and get-out-the-vote drives and on certain types of material used for volunteer activities. These monies could not be directed toward the campaign of any one candidate, but all party candidates would benefit from the overall efforts of party committees. The 1979 amendments were tinkering with the overall structure of the FECA. Congress has subsequently passed no further campaign finance legislation, even though several bills have been discussed, nor have the courts been inclined to reevaluate the *Buckley* decision.

The reforms launched by the FECA notwithstanding, campaign money continues to be an inflammatory issue today. Some say elections cost too much thus driving out impecunious candidates (Etzioni 1984). Others say PACs play an inordinate role in the electoral process, harming the parties and democracy (Drew 1983, Stern 1988). Critics also point out that the present system of campaign financing leads to a lack of competition in House races (Magleby and Nelson 1990).[5] Still others say money has always been part of the electoral process and that the situation is better today than at any time in the past (Sorauf 1988).

One issue seems to be beyond contention—money has an impact on the likelihood of candidate success or failure. Generally, the better funded candidate is the victor in most congressional elections. Incumbents have the advantage of incumbency, which generally provides access to more campaign funds than their opponents, leading to increased chances of re-election, especially in House races. Therein lies a tale, part of which is addressed later in this book.

The impact of money on congressional elections has been thoroughly investigated (e.g., Jacobson 1980, 1985, Sabato 1984, Sorauf 1988, Magleby and Nelson 1990). Gary Jacobson (1980) contends funding is crucial for candidate success in the political environment dating from the late seventies. Incumbents generally have little difficulty raising money, but their spending exhibits a declining marginal return. Because of advantages such as name recognition, incumbents have to spend less money than do challengers in order to be reelected, and additional spending beyond a minimum produces a small increase in the number of votes received. More recently, some scholars contend incumbent spending does have an impact on the vote percentage received (Green and Krasno 1988, 1990, Thomas 1989). Challengers, on the other hand, increase their vote totals with increased spending at all levels. There appears to be a floor of about $250,000 (Jacobson 1987, 1990) that challengers must achieve in order to be competitive. Challengers have difficulty raising funds and declining marginal returns applies to them too (Theilmann and Wilhite 1989). Incumbents have less difficulty raising money, but do not need to spend it as lavishly as do challengers or candidates in open-seat races who often outspend either incumbents or challengers. Jacobson (1980, 1990) contends that lavish spending by an incumbent is a sign of a strong challenge. His two-stage least squares (2SLS) regression model indicates that money influences electoral outcomes, but projected outcomes (i.e., candidate strength) influence the amount of money raised, a simultaneous relationship.

While the fortunes and actions of incumbents and challengers are intertwined in Jacobson's model, other commentators (Ragsdale and Cook 1987) call this relationship into question. Incumbent strength extends beyond fund-raising ability since incumbents already have more receipts; this in itself is a source of votes. Some challengers are prone to underestimate incumbent strength while overestimating their own chances, even when they have poor funding prospects (Kazee 1980). The strength of the incumbent partially determines the strength of the challenger, as incumbents perceived to be vulnerable are more likely to attract strong challengers, and challenger effort influences incumbent behavior. Lynn Ragsdale and T. E. Cook (1987) contend that their actions are relatively unrelated. Specifically, they maintain that strong challengers appear when the previous race included a strong challenger rather than when an incumbent's resources are perceived to be low. Moreover, incumbents use their resources based on previous patterns rather than on the perception of challenger action. Because Jacobson includes only financial resources in his calculations while Ragsdale and Cook include other resources, their approaches are not completely complementary. Incumbent and challenger financial resources may be related while their overall campaign resources may not display such a strong connection.

In addition to investigating the overall influence of money, Jacobson (1980, 1985) has examined the impact of PAC funds and party contributions in much the same fashion. He finds that political action committees pursue different and often conflicting objectives and hence do not achieve an inordinate influence over candidates. Commentators, such as James Herndon (1982), David Gopoian (1984), Laura Langbein (1986), Jean

Schroedel (1986), Diana Evans (1988), and Janet Grenzke (1989a) maintain that in certain circumstances PACs do achieve influence, especially if obtaining access rather than vote buying is an aim. Only a few PACs (mainly ideological ones) pursue a contrary course of backing challengers to hated incumbents in order to send a message, but if the National Conservative Political Action Committee's (NCPAC) fortunes in recent years are any indication, such a strategy is not very productive. Jacobson (1985–86) views the Republican Party as more efficient in its funding strategy in addition to having larger resources. Wilhite and Theilmann (1989) and Kevin Leyden and Stephen Borrelli (1990) have recently called this Republican efficiency into question, maintaining that it is simply the magnitude of Republican financial resources that is important. What seems to be clear is that most institutional sources of campaign money are more attracted to incumbents than to challengers, with open-seat candidates occupying a middle ground.

Most of the commentators whose work is discussed above are squarely in the pluralist political tradition that finds that although PACs may be powerful, their power is diluted by conflict with each other. Challengers may be underfunded relative to incumbents, but strong challengers can find campaign resources. Incumbents do not receive the benefits they may think they do from increased funding, but their advantages do not rest solely on a campaign war chest.

Elizabeth Drew's (1983) approach and conclusions are in direct contrast to the pluralist viewpoint. Her anecdotal work is a full-scale attack on the role of money, especially PAC contributions, in congressional elections. She bemoans the large sums being spent and contends competition for PAC funds helps shape senators' and representatives' voting decisions. Her views are amplified by Philip Stern (1988), who contends PAC contributions are only one means that interest groups have of influencing congressional voting, others being honoraria and lavish expenses paid to members of Congress for speaking to organizations, often in exotic locales.[6]

Drew's, Stern's and Amitai Etzioni's views may be close to the popular impression, but most sophisticated econometric research (e.g., Welch 1982, Chappell 1982, Wright 1985, Grenzke 1989b) does not support this conclusion. However, it does appear that there are occasions in which PAC funding does influence congressional voting (Kau, Keenan, and Rubin 1982, Wilhite and Theilmann 1987). Generally, PAC influence becomes detectable on small out-of-the-way measures that are not widely covered by the media (Schroedel 1986) and that do not have strong conflicting forces interested in them (Sabato 1984). This is not to say that political action committees are wasting their money; contributions buy an opportunity to influence congressional decisions at an early stage, if only at the margin; this is an opportunity denied most individuals.

A particularly interesting aspect of the rise of PACs has been the growth of those whose sole purpose is to engage in political activities. Most PACs are connected to a parent organization such as a labor union, a corporation, or an organization, such as the American Medical Association. Some PACs have no parent organization and are often responsible solely to their leadership committee, which may be an individual. Many, although not all, of the nonconnected PACs are ideological in nature, at times supporting one issue instead of the larger number of issues that most interest groups advocate (Latus 1984). As Frank Sorauf (1984–85, 1988) contends, these nonconnected organizations display the most potential for abuse. Because they have no parent organization to take responsibility for their actions, the nonconnected PACs are more likely in Sorauf's estimation to test the bounds of the FECA through such techniques as independent expenditures.

Perhaps because of the novelty of PACs or the notoriety of some, such as the NCPAC, more attention has been paid to this source of funds than to parties or individuals. In addition to dealing with the questions noted above, political scientists have examined the motivation for PAC contributions (e.g., Herndon 1982, Gopoian 1984, Masters and Delaney 1985, Masters and Keim 1985, Eismeier and Pollock 1986a) and PAC organization (Eismeier and Pollock 1985, 1988). Larry Sabato (1984) provides the most comprehensive examination of the PAC phenomenon, concluding that PACs are not harmful to the political process.

Little attention has been paid specifically to party contributions. This situation is partially due to the oft-lamented "decline" of the parties. Congressional candidates run their own campaigns, at times relegating the parties to a superfluous role. Generally, party behavior is examined as part of an overall attention to the parties' (e.g., Kayden and Mahe 1985) role in elections or as a theoretical construct by positive political theorists. Jacobson's (1985–86) and Al Wilhite and John Theilmann's (1989) work may open up further empirical consideration of the parties' financial activities. Herrnson (1988) argues that parties are starting to regain influence and become major financial players in the electoral process at the congressional level. David Magleby and Candice Nelson (1990) make this same point, particularly in regard to coordinated spending by party committees. Such spending is done by party committees independent of the candidate, for example, to encourage people to register to vote, or "stay the course" with the president's party. These measures can also benefit congressional candidates.

Individual contributory behavior too has received scant attention in spite of the fact that individual contributions continue to make up about 60 percent of the receipts of congressional candidates. No longer dominant, the "fat cats" have given way to the wizards of direct mail who promise to raise large sums for favored candidates. Organizations such as the Congressional Club raise large sums of money from individual contributors by direct mail albeit with extremely high overhead costs. Most studies of individual political behavior concentrate on voting or organizational membership rather than the act of making campaign contributions. Admittedly, a small percentage of the populace contributes money to congressional campaigns, but little has been done to assess the impact of this money aside from general models of the impact of campaign contributions (Jacobson 1980). One recent work (Theilmann and Wilhite 1989) raises some questions in comparing the contribution patterns of individuals and institutional sources.

A special case of individual funding is the candidate. Most challengers and candidates for open seats are forced to bear part of the cost of their campaigns directly or through loans (Wilcox 1988a). The fifty-one first-time winners of the 1984 House races spent, on average, $32,539 of their own resources. Such spending helps to establish a candidate's credibility as a serious candidate, making it easier to raise additional funds. The *Buckley* decision struck down the limit on candidates' contributions to their own campaigns. In 1984, Governor Jay Rockefeller won a Senate seat in West Virginia, personally providing $10.3 million of the slightly over $12 million spent in the contest. Two years earlier, Mark Dayton, a department store heir married to a Rockefeller grand-daughter, spent $6.8 million of his own money in a losing senatorial contest in Minnesota. Without other credentials, great wealth cannot guarantee victory. Candidates who cannot convince others to support them are usually weak candidates. As Sorauf puts it: " 'Losers' often are self-financed, and self-financed candidates are losers (1988, 68)." Incumbents, moreover, can raise sums to equal the war chests of all but the most determined multimillionare. In 1984, for example, eleven House candidates spent at least $200,000 of their own money; six lost in primaries and the other five lost in November. Conversely, the fifty-one first-time victors in 1984 contributed $32,539 to their own campaigns, but that amount was only 7.3 percent of their total receipts.

Today, campaign funding is a continuing headache for most candidates, although challengers and candidates in open-seat races feel the pressure most strongly. As Harriet Woods (the challenger for John Danforth's Senate seat in Missouri in 1986) put it: "The price for running for the Senate today is spending more time than you'd like to spend asking people for more money than they'd like to give (New York *Times Magazine*, 2 November 1986)." The same could be said about many House races. Even when they gain office, fund-raising is a continual chore for House members, leading to missed floor votes or committee meetings as members attend to fund-raising instead. The fund-raising dance is thus more subtle than simply buying votes. It affects the ability of members of Congress to carry out their duties on a daily basis.

With the large sums involved, what do the candidates spend the money on? Many of the expenses of the past, such as campaign buttons, bumper stickers, and other paraphernalia, account for only a small portion of the expenses of most congressional candidates in the 1980s. In some districts communication costs still involve substantial expenditures on billboards and radio. One old-fashioned method is still being used but with a different twist—letters to the voters. Today incumbents often deluge their constituents with mailings, especially during election years. The major innovation in letters to the voters has been the rise of the direct-mail wizards who have developed lists that enable candidates to target, say, Methodist, gun-owners, or more-lucrative groups such as veterans or the elderly (Godwin 1988). While part of the goal of direct mail is to pay for itself, its utilization is not cheap, and some candidates have found that overhead costs far outrun any advantages (Luntz 1988, 162). Television time, however, is an increasingly large expense for many congressional candidates. Communication costs have always been a major component in campaign budgets, but especially today. A typical consultant's advice is often to minimize administrative costs in order to spend the maximum part of the campaign budget on communications. The problem is that the growth rate for advertising costs has exceeded the growth rate of the consumer price index. Between 1976 and 1982, a period of rapid growth of campaign expenses, the McCann-Erickson index to media advertising costs rose 79 percent, while the Consumer Price Index rose 69 percent (Sorauf 1988, 342–43).

Another major component of campaign expenses involves administrative costs. Office expenses and personnel costs have always been part of campaigns, but inflation and the need to deal with larger constituencies has driven these costs up during the seventies and eighties. Another administrative cost involves complying with FEC and state disclosure regulations, an effort that takes staff time, computer time, and even legal expertise. With the declining ability of parties to provide support in these areas (and candidate desire for such support) individual candidates carry the burden of these expenses. Herrnson (1988) may well be right in maintaining that the parties are making a comeback in this area, but candidates will continue to shoulder much of the load.

A relatively new administrative cost facing congressional candidates is that of hiring expertise. At one time a candidate and her friends ran a campaign perhaps with help from or even supervision by a party. Now the first advice given to a prospective congressional candidate is to hire a consultant. House races generally do not involve the plethora of strategists, media consultants, pollsters, and fund-raisers often found in Senate and gubernatorial races, but most candidates hire some professional expertise, even if only on a part-time basis (Sabato 1981, Luntz 1988, Salmore and Salmore 1989). The news media, PACs, and probably even some voters consider candidates without consultants as less than serious contenders unless they are incumbents of long standing. Indeed, some PACs go as far as to consider the identity of the consultant when making contribution decisions (Luntz 1988, 45).

Some commentators might say candidates have driven up the demand for campaign funds artificially—that they do not need to spend so much on communications or consultants. Candidates might even agree orally, but few would wish to decrease their spending. While dollar expenditures sound staggering, political campaigns in the United States are less costly per-voter than those in West Germany, Ireland, and Israel (Penniman 1984, 51–53). Or compared in another way, in 1984 the total campaign cost of all national, state, and local races in the United States was $1.8 billion, but General Motors, Ford, and Chrysler spent $1.65 billion in advertising costs in the United States that same year (Sorauf 1988, 368). Is finding out about candidates worth as much as finding out about new car models? Some campaign spending may tell us little about the candidates' ability to govern, but the same type of criticism can be leveled at automobile advertising.

Although the growth rate of campaign costs may be leveling off, congressional elections already are expensive and are likely to become more so in spite of increasing calls for reform. Candidates who are unable or unwilling to raise large sums of money will be at a competitive disadvantage.

Studies of financial campaign activity generally have not considered the twin issues of racial and sexual discrimination. Other studies explore political activities of blacks and females, but those works show scant interest in campaign finances, and while funding is not the sole determinant of candidate success, it plays an important role. So too the candidate's race and sex appear to have an impact on electoral outcomes. By reviewing the largely separate investigations into race and sex versus campaign finances, our task is revealed: merging these issues.

NOTES

1. All contribution and spending figures for the 1980s are taken from the data tapes: Federal Election Commission, *FEC Reports on Financial Activity 1979–80, 1981–82, 1983–84, 1985–86, 1987–88: House/Senate.*

2. Extensive discussions of the ways in which congressional candidates spend their money are Barbara Salmore and Stephen Salmore (1989) and Magleby and Nelson (1990).

3. The expectation of support from bosses, such as Penrose, extended to the House since they were expected to control the congressional delegation in whole or part.

4. The FECA with its subsequent amendments and implementing regulations are found in Federal Election Commission, *Federal Election Campaign Laws*, January 1985, and 11 CFR 1.1, January 1985.

5. Magleby and Nelson (1990) provide the most comprehensive discussion of the need for finance reform, complete with a well thought out reform package. Their analysis is empirical instead of anecdotal. Sabato's (1989) discussion is less empirical, but he too emphasizes that PACs are only part of the finance problem.

6. In a recent discussion of campaign finance reform, Sabato (1989) calls for severe curtailment of honoraria, rather than PAC spending, emphasizing that honoraria have a greater potential for abuse than does PAC spending, which he characterizes as only "pseudo corruption."

Chapter Four

Aggregate Contributions in Theory and Practice

Blacks make up 12 percent of the U. S. population, but hold a mere 4 percent of congressional seats. Women hold about 5 percent of House seats even though they account for over half of the voting population. Reviewing a variety of explanations for this discrepency, we found that many became increasingly irrelevant during the seventies and eighties. An additional possibility that has not been adequately explored is the role of money. This chapter begins our investigation of the impact of money on the underrepresentation of women and blacks in Congress.

Numerous works investigate the impact of money on congressional campaigns, but only a handful (e.g., Uhlaner and Schlozman 1986, Burrell 1986, Wilhite and Theilmann 1986, Theilmann and Wilhite 1986) examine the impact of campaign funding on the election of blacks and women. As shown in chapter 3, underfunded candidates are likely to be unsuccessful candidates. In this chapter we examine the overall impact of funding on congressional campaigns. Subsequent chapters will subdivide campaign funds into individual, party, and PAC contributions and investigate racial and/or sexual bias by those sources of funds.

A quick look at aggregate campaign contributions shows a racial and sexual differential. Table 4.1 compares average campaign contributions for members of the House of Representatives by race and sex for the 1980–1988 election cycles.

The averages reported in Table 4.1 suggest women and blacks have been at a financial disadvantage in congressional races. In the 1980 election cycle, female candidates received about 80 percent of the funds that white male candidates received. That differential declined over the

Table 4.1
Average Campaign Contributions: House of Representatives

	white males	females	blacks
1980	$154,763	$125,058	$85,208
1982	$230,960	$203,902	$120,003
1984	$248,658	$227,109	$172,086
1986	$288,531	$245,198	$324,880
1988	$300,182	$356,753	$363,065

decade, and by 1988 average contributions to female candidates were greater, on average, than those to white male candidates. A similar phenomenon applies to black candidates as blacks received only 55 percent of the funds white males received in 1980, but by 1988 contributions to blacks were also larger, on average.

Summary statistics, however, mask many things, and conclusions about discrimination should not be drawn too quickly. For example, the existing literature suggests strong candidates are generally more successful in obtaining financial support.[1] The previously cited explanations for a lack of black and female candidates may also explain the contribution gap. If black or female candidates have a smaller chance of winning elections than do white males, their ability to raise money will also be affected. If females and blacks are less likely to win because voters are culturally biased, or if "racial gerrymandering" lowers their chance of success (Engstrom and Wildgen 1977), or if the differential is due to lower participation rates by blacks (Shingles 1981) which leads to weaker female or black candidates, then they will also receive less financial support from contributors even if contributors are not discriminating on the basis or race or sex. Funding shortfalls may follow electability differences instead of signaling a racial or sexual prejudice.

Among other things, this work differentiates between actual funding differentials caused by contributor bias and factors affecting candidate support. The challenge is to separate funding decisions based on the candidates' race and sex from decisions based on other electability traits considered important by contributors.

Why is this distinction important? Suppose for a moment that black and female candidates are in fact inferior candidates. Suppose further that contributors recognize this situation and invest less money in their election. We would thus observe the funding differentials found in the earlier years of Table 4.1. If this is the case, efforts to encourage increased funding for black and female candidates would accomplish little except to increase the probability that some of these "inferior" candidates would be elected. Clearly this is not socially optimal. On the other hand, a circular pattern may exist. If women and/or blacks are less likely to be elected, the quality of female and black candidates may drop, leading to the funding differentials of Table 4.1. In that case, better candidates will not surface until the funding inequities are erased. From another perspective, funding differentials have clear-cut impacts. Suppose we accept the very likely proposition that female and black candidates are just as capable, or incapable, as are white male candidates. In this scenario discriminatory funding differentials have sizable social costs because quality candidates, knowing they will be underfunded, are less likely to seek office or to be elected. Still, the source of this discrimination is not clear. Individual contributors or interest groups and political parties may be prejudiced and may be practicing direct discrimination. Likewise, contributors may not have prejudicial preferences, but they may have a perception that voters possess these views. Hence the skewed contributions displayed in Table 4.1 may reflect the indirect discrimination of rational, unbiased contributors reacting to the differing probabilities of winning.

Does it matter whether funding discrimination is direct, that is, contributors exercising their prejudices, or indirect, that is, contributors thinking voters are prejudiced, reducing their electibility and causing contributions to drop? Yes. It is through the identification of the origins of discrimination that remedies can be constructed to counteract it. Surely an effective policy depends on correctly identifying the source of the problem. For example, if black candidates receive less money because 30 percent of the population chooses to vote against any black candidate, one sort of remedy will be required. Contrast this scenario to a situation in which voters are quite willing to support black candidates, but blacks are underfunded and run weak races. Effective policies to counteract these inequities will differ because the origins and processes of discrimination are different.

As Table 4.1 shows, the total funding differential between black and white candidates was large at the beginning of the eighties, but it contains two distinct components. The first is direct discrimination that entails contributors who are culturally biased and who therefore reduce or eliminate contributions to black or female candidates because of their race and/or gender. The second component is indirect discrimination that may occur if contributions are based on a candidate's political attributes such as perceived chances of winning or political clout. If black and female candidates rank lower on these scales than do white candidates, they may receive fewer contributions for reasons other than race and sex.

To differentiate between these two influences, we need to explore campaign decisions by candidates and contribution decisions by contributors. These issues are explored theoretically in the next section, and then tested empirically. In the process an overview of the statistical relationship between aggregate contributions, spending, and votes emerges.

The next three chapters use variations of this general model to investigate specific sources of funds. Do political action committees discriminate on the basis of race and/or gender (chapter 5)? Do political parties (chapter 6)? Do individuals (chapter 7)? Through the exploration of these questions in the aggregate and within specific categories of contributions, the overall relationship of voter and contributor discrimination should become clearer.

A RENT-SEEKING MODEL OF THE POLITICAL CAMPAIGN

The theoretical model developed in this section is based on recent developments in the rent-seeking literature. Rent-seeking can be defined as the expenditure of resources for the purposes of capturing a preexisting value (Tollison 1982). Candidates campaigning for political office fit this description well. An election involves an expenditure of resources for the purpose of capturing a pre-existing value—the pay, power, and prestige of office. Contributors are also seeking rent by expending resources, campaign contributions, to obtain a preexisting value—influence over the legislative process. In either case the rent-seeking paradigm provides a convincing explanation of the behavior of candidates and contributors. Gordon Tullock (1980) presented a model of strategic rent-seeking in which two identical players, X and Y, are buying tickets for a lottery. Player X's purchases (x) relative to the total tickets held by both players (x + y) determines his or her probability of winning the prize, R. Player X's optimal strategy involves maximizing the expected value of playing or:

$$E(x) = \frac{x}{x + y}(R - x) + \frac{y}{x + y}(-x). \qquad (4.1)$$

Y's optimal strategy entails a similiar calculation. By maximizing E(x), Tullock derives reaction functions for each player and a Cournot-Nash equilibrium for the game. He also explores the ramifications of additional players, different functional forms, and bias.

The application of this general framework to political campaigns has a great deal of intuitive appeal. Campaigns are competitive games in which two or more candidates invest resources with the objective of increasing their probability of winning the contest. Measuring the effort put forth by two identical candidates as "x" and "y", the probability of candidate X winning an election is $x/(x + y)$, and a strategy focusing on the expected value of running for office yields equation (4.1).

Chris Paul and Al Wilhite (1990) derive a simple campaign model based on Tullock's structure by recognizing the role of third-party contributors. Central to their thesis is the concept that candidates exchange something in order to generate contributions.[2] Consider for the moment that political IOUs are given to contributors in return for their support. These IOUs can take many forms: vague promises of legislative action, more specific quid pro quo legislation, or an under-standing of accessibility to contributors. Regardless of their form, this exchange involves a contribution in return for some activity by the candidate if elected. Hence, third-party contributions impose costs because they restrict the latitude of elected candidates, reducing the office's net value.[3]

A key attribute of this model is that political IOUs are usually conditional. If a candidate wins, the promise is valid and can be collected by contributors. However, when a candidate loses, the IOU is voided. This leads to an asymmetric cost structure changing the game's solution. The expected value of a candidate in this regime is:

$$E\,(x) = \frac{x}{x + y}\,(R - x) - 0. \qquad (4.2)$$

Because third-party contributions purchase conditional IOUs, the second term drops out. An immediate result of this approach is that candidates relying on third-party contributions tend to invest greater resources than do candidates who finance their own campaigns. This increases the social cost of the game. Naturally, candidates can dissemble, by selling political IOUs during the campaign and reneging on the deal once elected. But the benefits of such behavior are short lived. Contributors (and voters) are likely to abandon these candidates, and their chances of re-election are small.

Several strategies dominate outright lying. One is to make vague rhetorical promises because these promises require no specific action on the part of the elected official and so their cost is low. Not surprisingly, they are often of little value to shrewd contributors and generate few campaign contributions. A particularly attractive version of this type of promise arises when a candidate can label an opponent as being pro-communist, antifamily, or possessing some other deplorable but vague characteristic. The implicit contract is that the candidate will do the contributor a favor by winning the election and keeping the opponent out of office. While this strategy is often difficult to accomplish, the returns are very large because unconstrained support follows a successful smear. The potentially large payoff of this strategy may help explain the prevalence of dirty campaigns.

Another fruitful approach is to concentrate on courting individuals and special-interest groups with political views close to the candidate's own. For example, suppose a candidate has a pro-union background and fully intends to support labor legislation; if she can secure union PAC contributions in return for pro-union stances, a position she would have taken anyway, there is little restriction on her latitude once elected.

By incorporating several amendments to Gordon Tullock's (1980) structure, we develop a more complete political rent-seeking model. First, an election bias, labeled e, recognizes that candidates possess different campaign capabilities. A primary distinction lies in candidates' initial endowment of political capital, such as name recognition or record, which varies across candidates. These differences lead to a bias in spending effectiveness, similar to a production efficiency. This election bias term is added as a scaler to X's spending. If $e > 1$, X possesses the election advantage, $e < 1$ signifies Y's advantage, and if $e = 1$ candidates possess equal amounts of political capital. In a more general formulation the parameter e would be a function of unspecified shape instead of the scaler adopted here, but this simpler approach is sufficient for this study.

Second, the value of an office being sought can differ across candidates. For example, an incumbent with seniority and existing political relationships may occupy a position of power such as a committee chair or a role in the party leadership. Hence, the value of the seat is larger for that individual. This office bias, o, is added to the model as a scaler on the rent value at stake for candidate X. If $o > 1$, X places a higher value on the seat, $o < 1$ if Y has the rent bias in his/her favor, and when $o = 1$ there is no bias.[4]

The assumption that all resources arise from third parties is also dropped. In this formulation, candidates can contribute time and money to their own campaign. This alternative source of funding enters the model through the addition of a parameter, α, which represents the proportion of spending collected from third-party contributors. As before, third-party contributors trade for IOUs that can be collected only if the candidate wins. The candidate's own contributions are lost, regardless of the electoral outcome.[5]

The value of political IOUs varies across candidates and contributors, and a price vector is entered to capture this distinction. The political price, p, of a specific third-party contribution depends on the candidates' ideology, the ideology of their constituencies, and their subjective probability of winning the election. For example, if a candidate with a pro-labor background is running for election in a district with a large organized labor population, the political price of a contribution from a labor PAC is quite small. Alternatively, the price required to obtain a corporate contribution could be politically prohibitive. Further, contributors' demands are likely to be inversely related to the candidate's probability of winning. An incumbent with a high probability of re-election will be able to generate financial support with vague promises to provide access. Long-shot challengers will have to offer the possibility of more-extensive cooperation or support.

After including these conditions in the candidates' decision calculus, the expected value of campaign expenditures for candidate X, equation (4.2) becomes:

$$E(x) = \frac{ex}{ex + y}(oR - p\alpha x - (1-\alpha)x) + \frac{y}{ex + y}(-(1-\alpha)x). \quad (4.3)$$

The first term on the right-hand side of equation (4.3) consists of the probability of winning the election (the relative resource commitments of each candidate and the bias accompanying those efforts) times the value of the elected office. The postelection value of the office consists of the initial rent (including any office bias), minus the price of third-party contributions times their size, minus the value of the candidate's own contributions. Contributions from the candidate are assigned a price of unity, and prices of third-party contributions are measured relative to that cost. If third-party contributions are less onerous than a candidate's own contributions, $p < 1$.

Including the possibility of candidates making contributions to their own campaigns changes the cost of losing the election. The second term on the right-hand side is no longer zero. If a candidate contributes $1,000 to her own campaign and loses (see n. 5), her money is lost. The second term then reflects the probability of losing the election times the amount of the candidate's own resources invested in the effort.[6]

Similarly, the expected value of spending by candidate Y equals:

$$E\,(y) = \frac{y}{ex + y}\,(R - p\alpha y - (1-\alpha)\,y) + \frac{ex}{ex + y}\,(-(1-\alpha)\,y). \qquad (4.4)$$

Maximizing equations (4.3) and (4.4) yields the optimal expenditures, x^* and y^*, for candidates X and Y.

$$x^* = \frac{-y\,(1 - \alpha + p\alpha) + \sqrt{(1 - \alpha + p\alpha)\,(p\alpha y^2 + eyrR)}}{e\,(1 - \alpha + p\alpha)}, \qquad (4.5)$$

and

$$y^* = \frac{-ex\,(1 - \alpha + p\alpha) + \sqrt{p\alpha e^2 x^2 + exR}}{(1 - \alpha + p\alpha)}. \qquad (4.6)$$

Candidate X's optimal campaign strategy depends on the spending of candidate Y, the rent value of the office, bias terms e and o, and the proportion of spending paid from the candidate's own pocket. Candidate Y is affected by the same factors.

Derivatives of these reaction functions predict relationships that are amenable to empirical testing. For example, the first derivative of x^* with respect to y, $\delta x^*/\delta y$, is positive, as is $\delta y^*/\delta x$. Candidates increase their effort in response to increased spending by their opponents. Second, the rent value of the office, R, and office bias, o, are both positively related to X's effort, and candidate Y behaves similarly: $\delta y^*/\delta R > 0$ and $\delta y^*/\delta o < 0$. A third implication is the impact of the election bias, e. While $\delta x^*/\delta e > 0$, $\delta y^*/\delta e < 0$. As one candidate gains an electability bias, that candidate's efforts diminish while the opponent increases his effort in an attempt to overcome the disadvantage. Further, the second derivatives, $\delta^2 x/\delta e^2$ and $\delta^2 x/\delta e^2$ are both negative, indicating the election bias has diminishing returns.[7]

The price of third-party contributions, p, and its relationship to spending and the proportion of a candidate's own funds leads to some interesting hypotheses. One, $\delta x^*/\delta p$ and $\delta y^*/\delta p$ are both negative. As third-party contributions become more expensive or require more-restrictive political promises, total spending declines. In economic terms this result is analogous to an increase in the price of an input reducing output.

Two, the price of third-party contributions affects the proportion of own spending, $(1 - \alpha)$. As the cost of third-party funds increases, a larger portion of the candidate's effort will be self-financed. Furthermore, the price vector, $p = (p_1, p_2, \ldots p_i)$, assigns a price to each potential third-party contribution reflecting the cost it entails. The derivative of each specific price with respect to spending is negative, and the proportion of funding from that source declines. This price vector and the impact of specific prices of third-party contributions will be of central interest when we investigate contributions from PACs and political parties.

In sum, candidates are driven by the spending decisions of their opponents, their political capital or ability to attract votes, their ability to raise third-party contributions, and the value of the office at stake. As candidates spend additional funds and invest in their campaigns, they hope to attract votes. The goal of the campaign, after all, is to win the election.

The positive relationship between votes and campaign expenditures is well documented (see Jacobson 1980, 1985). As contributors increase their contributions to a particular candidate, the candidate becomes increasingly viable, which in turn attracts more contributions. This relationship creates some empirical difficulties. Campaign spending affects votes, and the level of votes received affects the probability of winning, and that affects the level of contributions. Therefore an empirical model of spending and votes must allow for this simultaneity. In the next section we construct and evaluate such a model.

AN EMPIRICAL MODEL OF MONEY AND VOTES

Theory suggests the percentage of the vote received by candidates, the spending candidates undertake, and the campaign contributions received are simultaneously determined. Strong candidates (those with a high probability of winning) find it easy to raise funds to finance their campaigns. At the same time, these campaign funds and the services they buy increase the candidate's chance of winning, leading to higher ratings in public opinion polls, making it easier to raise additional money.

In this section we construct an empirical model allowing for this simultaneous determination of votes, spending, and contributions. In the process, several additional factors that have been identified as important attributes of candidates' ability to obtain votes or raise funds are also evaluated. After this empirical model is defined, the race and sex of candidates is included in the estimation to see how these characteristics affect contributions and votes.

The first step is to identify the primary determinants of voting behavior. Viewing an election as a rent-seeking game suggests the proportion of the vote received by a candidate in an equally matched contest depends on the spending of the candidate relative to the spending of his or her opponent as suggested in equation (4.3). This concept is included directly in our empirical model. The first explanatory variable is RATIO$, (this variable and all subsequent variables are fully defined in an appendix at the end of the book) which is the spending of the candidate divided by the spending of both candidates. As RATIO$ increases, one candidate's spending increases relative to the other candidate's spending. This increase in spending is expected to increase the percentage of the final vote received.

Not all candidates possess the same chance of winning because of different levels of name recognition, different political histories, and varied electoral records. Three variables measure the candidate's initial stock of political capital: the candidate's tenure in office, the square of this tenure figure, and performance in the previous campaign. Incumbents are extremely difficult to defeat. They have name recognition, an established campaign organization, the ability to affect certain events within their districts, and access to money that challengers usually lack. Further, as incumbents gain additional time in Congress, their advantages in these areas are expected to grow. Entering years in Congress (TENURE) captures the growing incumbency advantage, while its square (TENURE^2) allows for the possible nonlinearity of the influence. Specifically, this growing incumbency advantage may face diminishing returns.

Some incumbents, however, are less secure, and a predictor of their vulnerability is their percentage of the total vote (LASTVOTE) in the previous election. If an incumbent won the last election by a small margin, his constituents are probably dissatisfied, and the next race may attract a strong challenger. Unless the incumbent tends to constituent desires and ideology with greater zeal in the current term, he may be upset in the forthcoming election.

The remaining variables are dummy variables reflecting the candidate's race and sex, BLACK and FEMALE. These estimated coefficients are of central interest because they reflect voter discrimination. If voters are prejudiced against candidates who are black and/or female, these candidates will have a more difficult time winning elections, which could explain some of their funding differentials. Even though some contributors are voters in the district, dealing with contributor bias requires different remedies than does dealing with voter bias.

As with contributions, lower voting percentages for black and female candidates do not in themselves suggest voters are antifemale or anti-black. If voters perceive these candidates as being less likely to win, they may be reluctant to lend their support. The model constructed above allows us to control for this perception of a candidate's ability to win and to focus on contributor discrimination based on race or gender.

Some commonly discussed candidate traits are not included in this voting equation. For example, political pundits often discuss attributes such as charisma, being in step with the voters, aggressiveness, speaking ability, and television profile. These are undoubtedly important traits affecting elections. It is not necessary to measure and include this type of information explicitly because the importance of these characteristics is included indirectly. If a candidate has a winner's charisma, she likely has an advantage that is reflected in the above variables. Contributors recognize this advantage, public-opinion polls reflect this strength, campaign contributions rise, and the opponent's contributions do not. For candidates who ran in a previous election, these positive attributes affected that race and so their impact shows up in the previous voting percentage. There are unmeasurable, intangible factors affecting a campaign, and while the variables used in this model do not include them explicitly, these intangibles are included implicitly by measuring how voters and contributors react to the attributes directly included in the model. This method not only avoids a serious measurement problem, it captures the impact of central concern. We are not interested in candidates' charisma but in their electability.

A second equation explores campaign spending. Chapter 3 provides a review of the campaign spending literature, in which several relation-ships stand out. First, spending by either candidate increases as the race becomes tight. Using the resulting vote as a proxy for the expected vote, a variable called VOTEGAP, which is equal to $(\%\text{VOTE} - .5)^2$, measures the closeness of the race. This constructed variable ranges from 0 to .25. If each candidate receives exactly 50 percent of the vote (a very tight race), VOTEGAP $= 0$. In the most lopsided example, in which a candidate receives 100 percent of the vote, VOTEGAP equals .25 for both candidates. As the value of VOTEGAP grows, the race becomes increasingly lopsided, and a lopsided race is expected to generate less spending by both candidates, all else equal. Hence, the expected coefficient on VOTEGAP is negative. Because votes enter the spending equation and spending enters the voting equation, simultaneity is a possibility. In addition, both of these variables appear in the other equation in a nonlinear fashion. The estimation technique accounts for these complications.

Another variable reflecting the competitiveness of a race is a dummy variable for open-seat races (OPEN). Open-seat races are likely to attract strong candidates from both parties as well as the interest of funding sources. Because both candidates need to establish themselves before the electorate and each perceives a clear opportunity for victory, they are likely to spend large sums of money, money that is more likely to be more forthcoming than it would be if they were challengers. Even when a seat was held by a well-established incumbent, the race for succession is likely to be spirited as candidates of both parties expend maximum effort. For this reason the dummy variable OPEN is included as another close-race measure, one that is also indicative of the level of expenditures involved.

The third variable expected to affect a candidate's spending is the spending by the opponent. The derivatives of equation (4.3) suggest opposition spending is central to the spending decisions of a candidate. As an opponent spends increasing amounts of money (OPPONENT\$), the typical candidate is expected to increase his or her own spending in response.

The value of an elective office to a candidate (the office bias in equation [4.3]) is expected to affect candidate spending because if an office is worth more to one candidate he will spend more to acquire it, *ceteris paribus*. Two variables are included to measure dimensions of the value of an office. First, INCUMB is a dummy variable set equal to one for incumbents. Incumbents have developed political relationships and have gained seniority which increases their political power and adds to the value of an office. Simply put, the office is worth more to an incumbent, and she will spend money to defend her position. Similarly, being the chair or minority leader of a standing congressional committee, or holding other House leadership positions such as the Speakership, majority and minority leaders, or party whips, enhances the realm of influence and hence the value of the office for that candidate. The dummy variable COMMITTEE is included to measure the impact of these leadership positions.

The level of contributions received by a candidate (CONTRIBU-TION\$) is entered as a third equation. Contributors give money to candidates for a variety of reasons, but the primary forces can be captured with a few variables. Most contributors provide funds in the hopes that their contribution will help a candidate win the election. In many ways this motivation is misguided because given the minute effect any one contribution (even a large one) has on the total campaign fund, its impact approaches zero. This is much like the oft-discussed public-choice voting dilemma (see Brennan and Buchanan 1984), because a single vote will not affect an election but imposes costs, why do people vote? While the question as to why people vote or contribute money lies outside the scope of the current study, it is sufficient to observe that people do vote and people do contribute to campaigns.

In fact, contributions have other benefits making them economically rational. Contributions aid lobbying efforts (Sabato 1984, Jackson 1988, Wright 1990). If an interest group gains access to a representative because of a campaign contribution, then a contribution may have value regardless of its direct impact on the election.

In general, contributions are affected by two things: the candidates' desire for funds and their ability to raise money. The candidates' desire for contributions is well defined; contributions are used to finance campaign expenditures. Their demand for funds is not unlimited because each contribution carries with it an IOU and the cost in time and effort spent raising that money. There is an optimal level of candidate spending, given by equations (4.5) and (4.6), and this optimal spending drives the desire for contributions. The first variable in the CONTRIBUTION$ equation is therefore SPEND$.

While spending strategies help define how much money a candidate wants to raise, candidates are constrained by their ability to raise money from various sorts of contributors. In making their decision to support a particular candidate, contributors are motivated by a variety of factors derived from candidate characteristics and effort. For instance, one of the motives for contributions is to obtain access to representatives. A candidate who fails to win election to Congress can provide no access, and so contributors are expected to be concerned with the probability of victory. The percentage of the vote a candidate received in the previous election or the percentage of the vote received by the party's candidate in the preceding election for nonincumbents gives an indication of a candidate's strength to contributors. A big winner in the previous election is expected to win once again, and this makes contributions relatively easy to obtain.

Incumbency and congressional leadership positions reflect increased influence in the House. Contributors, anxious to receive some political benefit, are often likely to support powerful candidates. Because contributors view certain candidates as better investments in terms of power in the House, spending is included directly in the contributions equation to capture this effect. Incumbency and congressional leadership variables are included in the spending equation because incumbents and committee chairs and House leaders have more at stake than challengers or candidates for open seats and should be willing to expend considerable effort to maintain their position.

The remaining variables indicate the candidate's party affiliation, race, and sex. The Democratic dummy variable, DEMOCRAT, reflects the inherent funding differentials of the two parties. In addition to pointing up differences in resources and funding strategies regarding black and female candidates, it is necessary to include party affiliation because black candidates are disproportionately Democrats. Its exclusion would confuse party effects with race and sex differentials.

Estimated coefficients on the race and sex variables, BLACK and FEMALE, should reflect the amount of discrimination practiced by contributors after the impacts of the above variables have been taken into account. While total contributions may be lower for blacks and/or women in the aggregate, this does not necessarily mean contributors discriminate on the basis of race or gender. These candidates may not be as strong as their opponents. If voters discriminate against blacks and women, their chance of winning decreases, leading in turn to lower contributions. In this case, contributors could be more accurately described as discriminating against weak candidates, not against black or female candidates.

The complete model, a five-equation nonlinear simultaneous system, is formally stated below. In addition to the three equations described above, two identities are included that define the nonlinear relationship between votes and spending. The first three equations (4.7, 4.8, 4.9) contain parameters to be estimated, and the predicted signs of their coefficients appear in parentheses below the variable names.

$$\%\text{VOTE} = f \underset{(+)}{(\text{RATIO}\$,} \underset{(+)}{\text{LASTVOTE},} \underset{(+)}{\text{TENURE},} \underset{(-)}{\text{TENURE}^2,} \underset{(?)}{\text{BLACK},} \underset{(?)}{\text{FEMALE}).} \quad (4.7)$$

$$\text{SPEND}\$ = g \underset{(-)}{(\text{VOTEGAP},} \underset{(+)}{\text{OPEN},} \underset{(+)}{\text{OPPONENT}\$,} \underset{(+)}{\text{INCUMB},} \underset{(+)}{\text{COMMITTEE}).} \quad (4.8)$$

$$\text{CONTRIBUTION}\$ = h \underset{(+)}{(\text{SPEND}\$,} \underset{(+)}{\text{LASTVOTE},} \underset{(+)}{\text{INCUMB},} \underset{(+)}{\text{COMMITTEE},}$$
$$\underset{(-)}{\text{DEMOCRAT},} \underset{(?)}{\text{BLACK},} \underset{(?)}{\text{FEMALE}).} \quad (4.9)$$

$$RATIO\$ = SPEND\$ / (OPPONENT\$ + SPEND\$). \qquad (4.10)$$

$$VOTEGAP = (\%VOTE-.5)^2 \qquad (4.11)$$

The first variable on the right-hand side of equation (4.7), RATIO$, measures the size of a candidate's campaign chest relative to all spending in the campaign. As suggested above, candidates with greater financial resources are generally able to obtain a greater percentage of the vote, and so the estimated coefficient is expected to be positive. The second indication of candidate strength is tenure in Congress. Incumbents win with greater regularity than do challengers, hence this coefficient is expected to be positive. If incumbency has diminishing returns, as we expect, the coefficient of $TENURE^2$ will be negative. The percentage of the vote obtained by the candidate in the last election, LASTVOTE, reflects two different types of candidate strength. First, a candidate who won by a large margin in the last election probably embodies characteristics that are conducive to winning and may be expected to win again. Second, a large winning margin in the last election discourages challengers, and so the opposition is probably weak. All else equal, candidates who did well in their last race are likely to be tough to unseat in the current election.

The estimated coefficients on the last two variables in equation (4.7) will reflect the degree of racial and sexual discrimination by voters. Because other variables in equation (4.7) control for the candidate's electability, opposition strength, and funding, any remaining differences in voting percentage appear to be a product of racial or sexual discrimination.

The first variable on the right-hand side of equation (4.8), VOTEGAP, reflects the tightness of the race. It is the appearance of VOTEGAP in the spending equation and of spending in the voting equation that gives this model its simultaneous nature. Votes affect spending and spending affects votes. However, the relationship is not linear. Votes affect spending in the nonlinear VOTEGAP identity (equation 4.11), and spending enters the voting equation through the RATIO$ definition given in equation (4.10). The expected sign of VOTEGAP is negative. The other tight-race measure, OPEN, is expected to have a positive coefficient.

The opposition's expenditures, (OPPONENT$) is expected to have a positive impact on spending as the theoretical model, equations (4.5) and (4.6), suggests. Finally, candidates are expected to campaign more vigorously (and attract funds more readily) if their seat is one of greater influence. Because of seniority and political connections it is expected that incumbents, especially those in leadership positions in the House, will be able to spend more money than their opponents can, and positive coefficients are predicted for the variables, INCUMB and COMMIT-TEE.

Contributions, equation (4.9), are determined by the candidates' demand for funds and their ability to generate contributions. In this model the demand for contributions is defined by spending, and a positive sign for the variable SPEND$ is expected. Naturally constraints on spending arise primarily from a candidate's inability to raise money. For this reason the candidate's political clout, measured by incumbency, electorial record (LASTVOTE) and leadership position held (COMMITTEE), is expected to be related positively to contributions. Some contributors are interested in having access to powerful legislators after an election, and contributions are one avenue to access. Since incumbents have more seniority and better internal channels of power than do freshman legislators, incumbents are expected to receive greater support. Similarly, the ranking members of House committees and the Speaker, majority and minority leaders, and whips are expected to receive more money, *ceteris paribus*. Democratic candidates have traditionally raised less money than have Republican candidates, leading to a prediction of a negative sign for the DEMOCRAT coefficient.[8]

The estimated coefficients on the race and sex dummy variables reflect the level of racial and sexual discrimination on the part of contributors. Other explanatory variables in this funds equation control for the indirect discrimination component of the funding differential that is an overall reflection of candidate strength. Coefficients on these race and sex dummy variables reflect direct discrimination. It is the size and significance of these coefficients that will give us insight into funding inequities and perhaps illuminate methods to eliminate them.

DETERMINANTS OF AGGREGATE CONTRIBUTIONS

The empirical model outlined in equations (4.7)–(4.11) is estimated using a nonlinear two-stage least squares approach (n2SLS), (see Judge, Hill, Griffiths, Lutkepohl, and Lee 1982). The estimated parameters for the five House elections taking place from 1980 through 1988 are presented in tables 4.2 through 4.4.

In the voting equation, the coefficient on RATIO$, the ratio of the candidate's spending to total spending, is positive and strongly significant in all five election cycles. While the importance of spending in elections has been recognized for some time, the rent-seeking approach used here incorporates spending in a unique way. Focusing on the ratio of spending not only yields a strongly significant coefficient, it substantially increases the explanatory power of the voting equation. As a candidate spends more relative to her opponent, the percentage of the vote received increases substantially.

The second variable, LASTVOTE, also has a positive and significant coefficient in all five elections. Candidates who won by a large margin in the previous election do well in the current election. As is generally accepted, incumbents reflect constituent desires and benefit from voter inertia. In addition, incumbents are further advantaged by their status as some potentially strong challengers are discouraged from taking on an entrenched incumbent and leave the race to weaker candidates.

The tenure variables, TENURE and TENURE^2 usually have the expected signs, but TENURE is significant only in 1982 and TENURE^2

Table 4.2
Estimated Parameters for Vote Percentages—(Equation 4.7)

	1980	1982	1984	1986	1988
intercept	.1572**	.1729**	.1527**	.1580**	.1676**
	(.0086)	(.0088)	(.0094)	(.0086)	(.0085)
RATIO$	.4977**	.4012**	.4784**	.5672**	.4534**
	(.0304)	(.0251)	(.0258)	(.0277)	(.0266)
LASTVOTE	.1817**	.2395**	.2317**	.1333**	.2227**
	(.0310)	(.0259)	(.0329)	(.0292)	(.0304)
TENURE	.0013	.0043**	-.0007	.0013	.0005
	(.0018)	(.0016)	(.0016)	(.0017)	(.0016)
TENURE^2	-.00002	-.00006	.00003	-.00005*	-.00003
	(.00006)	(.00006)	(.00005)	(.00003)	(.00004)
BLACK	.0254	-.0138	-.0034	.0258	.0566**
	(.0187)	(.0157)	(.0162)	(.0201)	(.0202)
FEMALE	.0069	.0021	-.0135	-.0055	-.0090
	(.0138)	(.0131)	(.0119)	(.0124)	(.0130)
adj. R^2	.80	.79	.84	.83	.84

Standard errors lie below the estimated coefficients in parentheses. Significance at the .05 α-level is indicated by * and significance at .01 is represented by **.

only in 1986. In 1982, TENURE was positively related to votes received as long-term incumbents did well against challengers, while in 1986 diminishing returns seem to have set in for incumbents.

In only one election did the race and/or sex of a candidate have a significant impact on the percentage of the vote received. In 1988 it appears voters voted for black candidates in preference to white candidates, but there is no election in which the sex of the candidate has a significant impact on the percentage of the vote received. With the exception of 1988, there is not a case in which a race or sex coefficient is even close to significance at commonly accepted α-levels. This result is of particular interest because it suggests voters are not prejudiced, in the aggregate, in the voting booth. This may have important ramifications on the sources of funding differentials, if such differentials arise.

Table 4.3 presents results of the spending equation. The coefficient of the principal close-race measure, VOTEGAP, has the expected negative sign and is strongly significant in all five elections. As an election becomes increasingly tight, spending increased as both candidates invested increasing sums in the race. While there is an upward trend for VOTEGAP throughout the decade, note that the size of the coefficient is particularly large in the two off-year elections of 1982 and 1986, reflecting the flow of money into congressional races in nonpresidential election cycles. This result is especially evident in 1986. The emphasis that candidates place on open-seat races is evident from the OPEN measure as it is positive and significant for all five races. The importance of candidate spending is evident as open-seat candidates spent nearly $83,000 more than did other candidates in 1980, and this spending gap had increased to nearly $313,000 by 1988.

The opponent's spending, OPPONENT$, is also positive and strongly significant in all five election cycles. As the optimal spending strategies in equations (4.5) and (4.6) suggest, candidates respond to increased spending by an opponent with increased spending of their own. Specifically, an additional dollar of spending by an opponent led the candidate to spend another forty to fifty-five cents.

The last two variables, INCUMB and COMMITTEE, reflect the value of the election to the candidate. Both of these variables were expected to have a positive impact on spending as candidates with these attributes had more to gain from a victory and more to lose from a defeat than did their counterparts. The incumbency variable upheld this expectation as its coefficient was positive and significant in all five election years. Indeed, incumbents spent between $118,000 to $250,000 more than

Table 4.3
Estimated Parameters for Spending—(Equation 4.8)

	1980	1982	1984	1986	1988
intercept	27.351**	47.029**	-5.371	32.237*	-33.444*
	(9.703)	(14.029)	(13.999)	(19.199)	(19.146)
VOTEGAP	-485.435***	-674.213**	-600.339**	-992.440**	-819.881**
	(81.576)	(116.407)	(97.044)	(126.344)	(116.041)
OPEN	82.785**	140.075**	192.638**	260.349**	312.739**
	(15.975)	(19.295)	(24.290)	(25.982)	(31.114)
OPPONENT$	.5296**	.4149**	.5224**	.3786**	.4663**
	(.0300)	(.0318)	(.0307)	(.0330)	(.0315)
INCUMB	118.398**	216.942**	268.272**	307.115**	336.659**
	(9.672)	(16.564)	(12.902)	(18.262)	(18.149)
COMMITTEE	16.086	-20.044	4.708	25.154	-23.094
	(17.175)	(12.729)	(24.652)	(33.536)	(29.821)
adj. R^2	.41	.35	.47	.40	.48

Standard errors lie below the estimated coefficients in parentheses. Significance at the .05 α-level is indicated by * and significance at .01 is represented by **.

nonincumbent candidates on the whole. Leadership positions, however, were statistically unimportant.

Contributions' results appear in Table 4.4. Contributions are expected to be determined by the candidates' need for campaign funds and their ability to obtain them. Spending strategies, estimated in equation (4.8), define the need for funds, and the coefficient on this endogenous variable (SPEND$) is expected to be positive. This expectation is also confirmed as the coefficient on spending is positive and highly significant in all five election cycles.

A major constraint on fund-raising is the candidates' ability to raise money. Several variables were included to provide an indication of structural influences contributors consider when evaluating whether to contribute to a particular candidate. The percentage of the vote received in the last election and incumbency are both indications of candidate strength that many contributors consider favorably. In all five races both of these variables have the expected positive coefficients and are significant. Holding a leadership position in the House had mixed results with

Table 4.4
Estimated Parameters for Contributions—(Equation 4.9)

	1980	1982	1980	1986	1988
intercept	1.9915	2.1745	-1.0872	1.4685	.2528
	(2.1782)	(3.7762)	(4.9094)	(4.6732)	(6.217)
SPEND$	.9740**	.9299**	.9487**	.9565**	.9357**
	(.0078)	(.0110)	(.0116)	(.0106)	(.0145)
LASTVOTE	16.6034**	33.8803**	43.3047**	23.6024**	24.2990
	(4.7891)	(7.3582)	(11.0851)	(10.2799)	(15.3184)
INCUMB	11.8785**	19.8905**	32.2086**	37.1805**	43.2873**
	(2.3211)	(3.8312)	(4.8046)	(4.8128)	(7.8397)
COMMITTEE	.0510	-5.2311*	21.8154**	25.2327**	30.4146**
	(3.1751)	(2.686)	(6.9216)	(7.2781)	(9.7158)
DEMOCRAT	-5.0164**	-.5059	-7.9964**	1.6807	13.1699**
	(1.644)	(2.5164)	(3.1871)	(3.3139)	(4.8679)
BLACK	-7.6075*	-14.3741**	-22.0490**	-2.5055	-29.7918*
	(4.3911)	(6.0252)	(8.0683)	(9.9507)	(14.0761)
FEMALE	-3.3031	-2.3180	2.1222	-3.1799	1.3666
	(3.2168)	(4.9387)	(5.8835)	(6.0955)	(9.0366)
adj. R^2	.92	.89	.90	.93	.89

Standard errors lie below the estimated coefficients in parentheses. Significance at the .05 α-level is indicated by * and significance at .01 is represented by **.

coefficients usually possessing the correct sign, and being statistically significant in four cases. Generally contributors were supportive of the congressional leadership, indicating a desire to have friends in positions of power in the House. The Democrat dummy variable confirms the traditional partisan funding differential with a negative coefficient in three of the five election cycles. Running as a Democrat led to a shortfall of contributions ranging from $5,000 to $13,000. This relationship also may reflect the strength at the top of the ticket since Democratic shortfalls occurred in presidential election years, races in which strong Republican candidates dominated the top of the ticket.

The results show racial funding differentials, but little if any discrimination on the basis of sex by contributors. The coefficient on the black variable was negative in all elections and significantly so in four of the five cases. The size of the shortfall ranged from a low of $7,000 to a high of nearly $30,000. Apparently, being a black candidate in 1988 reduced a candidate's campaign contributions by nearly $30,000. This differential exists after we have accounted for most of the major candidate quality differentials. This differential is in contrast to the results reported in Table 4.1 that seemed to indicate that black candidates were doing well in the contest to raise campaign funds by the latter half of the eighties. The major source of this illusion is that in 1988 most black candidates were incumbents and because incumbents do well, average contributions to black candidates were high. Our regression results reveal a clearer picture; comparing like candidates, skin color matters. Female candidates fared better in the eighties. While four of the five estimated coefficients on the FEMALE variable were negative, none was significant at the .05 α-level.

AGGREGATE CONTRIBUTIONS ONLY A PARTIAL ANSWER

Using a rent-seeking model to investigate a candidate's optimal strategy for campaign expenditures has led to several testable hypotheses. Candidates are expected to spend more money in response to their opponents' spending, the value of the office, and their own electability traits. With this theoretical core in place, expectations concerning votes and contributions received were then generated. While many of the hypotheses are replicated in other empirical works, this chapter provides a sound theoretical foundation for some previously explored conjectures. The nonlinear specification employed here increases the explanatory power of the model.

Unique to this empirical model was the inclusion of a contributions equation in addition to the spending equation. Contributions were expected to be dependent on candidates' need for funds and their ability to raise money. The inclusion of the contribution equation allows us to explore funding differentials in a complete simultaneous system involving votes, spending, and contributions.

In general, the estimated parameters were consistent with the hypotheses forwarded here and in the existing literature. Votes received and campaign dollars spent are simultaneously determined, and the resulting spending desires are a primary determinant of total contributions. Strong candidates are more successful at raising money, and by spending these funds they receive additional votes, which translates into more money in subsequent elections.

With a successfully defined empirical model, further issues concerning candidates' race and sex can be addressed. While there is no theoretical reason for blacks or women to receive fewer votes or less money, prejudice may lead to that result. The results presented here suggest voters do not appear to discriminate on the basis of race and/or sex in the voting booth. In all five House election cycles studied, the race and sex of the candidate had no statistically discernable impact on the final voting percentages. In short, voter bias does not appear to be a viable explanation for the existing underrepresentation of blacks and women in Congress.

On the other hand, there does seem to be a pattern of racial discrimination in the allocation of total campaign contributions. After controlling for attributes such as candidate strength, opposition strength, party affiliation, and the incumbency advantage, black candidates received substantially lower levels of funds than did nonblack candidates. Because the primary determinants of candidates' fund-raising abilities are included in the analysis, the differential appears to be racially motivated.

Results for female candidates are less dramatic. In all five election cycles there was no discernible funding differential between male and female candidates. As is the case with black candidates, there are still unanswered questions here regarding the sources of money for women who run for Congress, questions we address later.

These results raise additional questions; one of the more perplexing is, if voters do not discriminate on the basis of race and sex, then why do contributors? This question will be explored by investigating particular sources of campaign funds. Each of the following chapters concentrates on a particular category of contributions, identifies the primary motivations of these contributors, and then measures potential racial and sexual discrimination. This disaggregation begins with a relatively new category of campaign funds, those generated by PACs, and is followed by an analysis of party contributions in chapter 6 and individual contributions in chapter 7.

NOTES

1. The campaign advantages flowing from campaign contributions are described by Jacobson (1980, 1985), Sorauf (1988), and Magleby and Nelson (1990), and the references therein.

2. Others have used the exchange paradigm; for example, George Stigler (1972) views candidates and voters as balancing the costs and benefits of actions. James Kau, Donald Keenan, and Paul Rubin (1982) suggest candidates maximize the probability

of being elected by balancing the wishes of contributors and voters, while Bender (1986) phrases a capital-theory approach in supply and demand terminology.

3. The value of an elected office includes the discounted value of its salary and the general ability to extract rents.

4. To simplify some of the algebra, e and r are assumed $\geq$ 1, so candidate X is defined as the "advantaged" candidate.

5. In actuality, successful candidates will be likely to recover expenditures made on their own campaigns, often from postelection PAC contributions (Wilcox 1988a).

6. While the candidate's financial cost may be high, the opportunity cost of the time spent campaigning is substantial as well.

7. Previous theoretical models (Kau, Keenan, and Rubin 1982, Jacobson 1980) assume the sign of these derivatives based on the expectation of diminishing returns. That is not necessary in this formulation.

8. Individual Democratic incumbents, however, have appeared to do very well in raising money from PACs in the latter half of the eighties (Jackson 1988). The implications of this situation are explored in chapter 5.

Chapter Five

Political Action Committees and Candidate Funding

The early 1970s witnessed a rapid evolution of campaign finance rules as legislation and judicial decisions spurred the establishment of PACs. A plethora of studies have examined several aspects of PAC behavior and the impact of their contributions, but few have explored the question of racial or sexual bias; Burrell (1985), Carol Uhlaner and Kay Schlozman (1986), Theilmann and Wilhite (1986), and Wilhite and Theilmann (1986) are the exceptions.

Campaign contributions from PACs have changed the structure of congressional campaigns. PAC money continues to grow more rapidly than do other sources of funds so as to make up an increasing share of total funds. Perhaps more crucial than the overall growth of PAC money is the overwhelming proportion of incumbent contributions made up by PAC money. While individual contributions remain the largest source of funds in the aggregate, they are no longer the most important source of funds for many members of Congress. Table 5.1 gives a summary of PAC contributions in absolute terms and as a percentage of total contributions through the eighties.

These summary statistics illustrate a steady growth in PAC money in absolute and relative terms. In 1980, average PAC contributions to candidates for the House of Representatives were about $45,000, a little over one-fourth of the total. By the end of the decade, the average had almost tripled to $122,000. This rate of growth outpaced increases in total contributions, and in 1988 almost a third of all contributions to congressional candidates were from political action committees.

Table 5.1
Overview of PAC Contributions in the 1980s

	1980	1982	1984	1986	1988
ALL CANDIDATES					
average PAC contributions	$45,000	$69,000	$90,000	$104,000	$122,000
percent of total contributions	26.5%	29.1%	32.9%	31.3%	32.5%
INCUMBENTS					
average PAC contributions	$65,000	$102,000	$139,000	$165,000	$196,000
percent of total contributions	39.5%	39.1%	45.5%	46.6%	48.6%
CHALLENGERS					
average PAC contributions	$27,000	$40,000	$40,000	$47,000	$43,000
percent of total contributions	17.3%	22.9%	22.7%	18.9%	17.8%

The growth in PAC money, while rapid, has been uneven. First, sources of PAC contributions have changed substantially during the decade. Labor PACs, which numbered 297 and contributed $13.2 million to House and Senate candidates (24 percent of total PAC contributions), were imposing players in 1980, reflecting their early start in organization. By 1988, there were 401 labor PACs, which contributed $41.2 million, and this figure stood at 26 percent of the total PAC contributions. While corporate PACs grew steadily in number and total contributions during the eighties, nonconnected PACs displayed the most rapid rate of growth, with 374 PACs contributing $4.9 million (9 percent of the total) in 1980 and 1,341 PACs contributing $20.3 million (13 percent of the total PAC contributions) in 1988, a 314 percent growth rate (derived from *Federal Election Commission Record*, August 1989). Finally, a recent trend for political action committees is to use independent expenditures instead of contributions to support favored candidates or oppose opponents (Sorauf 1988).

As important as the source of political action committee funds is, our interest is in their dispersion. Both incumbents and challengers received greater aggregate contributions from PACs in 1988 than in 1980, but the proportion of total funds made up of PAC money had become much larger for incumbents. PAC contributions to nonincumbents grew by 60 percent, $27,000 to $43,000 from 1980 to 1988, but PAC contributions to incumbents increased by more than 300 percent over the same period. PAC money accounted for 17 percent of nonincumbents' campaign chests in 1980 and had changed little, to 18 percent, by 1988. Tripling the incumbents' contributions increased the relative importance of PAC money so that by the end of the decade PAC contributions were nearly half (48.6 percent) of incumbents' total contributions.

It is unlikely the growing concentration of PAC money has been random; indeed, intuition suggests it is the result of a deliberate process. This chapter presents a theoretical model of PAC contributions, tests its predictions empirically, and investigates the consequences of PAC decisions to see if there is evidence of racial or sexual bias.

A THEORETICAL MODEL OF PAC CONTRIBUTIONS

Political action committees are a major tool for special interest groups. Indeed, a unifying characteristic of the diverse array of PACs is that their existence arises from political interests shared by a group. In other words a PAC arises when political issues define a special interest group that then uses campaign contributions to forward the group's objectives.[1] This political commonality allows us to structure a theoretical model of PAC contributions.

In chapter 4 we assumed candidates are rational economic decision makers who pursue contributions and formulate spending decisions based on the probable costs and benefits involved. In this chapter we assume political action committees are endowed with the same intelligence. PAC contributions are recognized as being costly, and decision makers allocating funds to candidates do so selectively as they weigh the cost of a contribution to a candidate against the benefits the contribution is expected to provide. PAC decision makers possess a set of political objectives, and the benefits of contributions flow from the pursuit of those goals. For this reason, contribution decisions made by PACs can be viewed as an investment.

The investment paradigm is useful because it deals with choices. Just as the construction of an investment portfolio entails selection among many assets to optimize an investor's financial objectives, the allocation of a PAC's resources is expected to optimize its chances of attaining its political objectives. In addition to allocating campaign funds to congressional candidates, interest group members have other methods available to pursue their goals. For example, an interest group might choose to concentrate its efforts on a public education effort, its members could choose some personal action (such as a letter-writing campaign) pursue state or local politics as an avenue with potential, or there may be a chance for judicial action. In any case alternatives exist for these political players; they will participate in a particular activity as long as its promise is greater than the alternatives.[2] Because several routes can further a particular objective, the "best" decision may not always be apparent. In this type of situation we assume PAC decision makers optimize their efforts by balancing the benefits of a decision against its cost.

PAC decisions are complicated by uncertainty and that many costs are opportunity costs (i.e., the cost of one decision is that those resources cannot be committed to other options).[3] With imperfect information and random disturbances in the system, the optimal strategy will usually be a mix of several options. This is what we typically observe with interest groups pushing on several pressure points at a time.

An example of this multifaceted strategy is the National Rifle Association's (NRA) typical reaction to proposed gun control legislation in Congress. Even before a bill is filed, NRA lobbyists spring into action, contacting individual members of Congress while its publicists churn out advertising copy, and individual NRA members are urged to contact their representatives and senators. Contributions of the NRA Political Victory Fund figure into this equation as a means of ensuring access by punishing enemies and supporting friends. Unlike immediate stategies directed to particular pieces of legislation, PAC contributions are usually part of a long-term strategy, as they seem to be effective in gaining access for organization representatives (Langbein 1986).

The situation outlined above is analogous to the problem faced by investors. Theoretical finance models treat investment decisions as being made at the margin, considering trade-offs between risk and return. A similar framework can be established for political contributions where a PAC balances the returns of a political question with the cost and uncertainty of achieving a political goal.

Supporters of a piece of legislation calculate its value through some process such as summing the benefits accrued to group members. In the absence of uncertainty it pays for a PAC to base its contribution calculation on the present value of these benefits. This present value incorporates the time dimension of the project (it takes time to execute a program and benefits accrue over its lifetime). However, this type of investment is not made under conditions of certainty, and optimal PAC contributions are affected by this risk.

The risks of a political venture are considerable. First, there is no guarantee a particular piece of legislation will ever arise during a particular congressional term. This may be a more serious concern for a PAC with a narrow agenda because most legislation is of little interest to it. If during a particular congressional term no legislation addresses the PAC's issue, access to members of Congress is relatively unimportant. Many PACs, however, are interested in a range of topics, and some legislation touching their interests will undoubtedly arise in every session. In these cases the legislative uncertainty involves the degree of importance for a particular term.

Second, PACs invest in candidates who may not win election or re-election to Congress. As the previous chapter demonstrated, support of a losing candidate is particularly expensive for an interest group because political IOUs are void when a candidate loses.[4] This type of uncertainty prompts most PACs to channel contributions to incumbents (e.g., Conway 1986, Eismeier and Pollock 1988). Open-seat candidates are better bets than are challengers and so are also attractive to risk-averse PACs. Jacobson (1985) and Keith Poole, Thomas Romer, and Howard Rosenthal (1987) suggest incumbents in close races may be particularly attractive to PACs because their contributions will be noticed and appreciated by candidates.

A third source of uncertainty involves the level of support a specific representative gives to an issue. Supporters and opponents of an issue vary a great deal in their desire and their ability to further a legislative agenda. Senior members of the House, especially those in leadership positions, have more opportunities to influence legislation than do other representatives, and so PAC managers are often faced with the challenge of balancing power and intensity of support when making contribution decisions or contacting members of Congress. The problem of identifying the quality of support acquired by a particular contribution is a major source of this uncertainty.[5]

In his examination of political action committees, Sabato (1984) outlines a similar view, although his interest in PACs is considerably different from ours. Sabato is concerned with the formation and general goals of PACs rather than with specific contribution decisions, hence he does not use the financial paradigm adopted here.

Still the uncertainty categories in equation (5.1) apply to both the formation of a PAC as well as decisions on the level of support. For example, the legislative uncertainty discussed here is echoed by Sabato as he addresses the formation of PACs, "perhaps the most powerful element (to form a PAC) is that the government concerns some industries more directly than others (1984, 30)." Theodore Eismeier and Philip Pollock (1985, see also Wilcox 1988b) include in their list organizational goals, constituency influences, decision-making patterns, and inter-organizational relations as variables affecting the decision to form a political action committee.

Many PAC directors see themselves as an extension of the parent organization's lobbying efforts. This situation is particularly true of organizations with Washington offices (Sorauf 1984, Eismeier and Pollock 1985). As part of a lobbying effort, PAC contributions are designed, at least in part, to ensure access to members of Congress by an organization's representatives. For example, representatives of groups who neglected to make contributions to Representative Tony Coelho's campaign committee or the Democratic Congressional Campaign Committee, which he chaired, often encountered a frosty reception when they tried to meet with him (Jackson 1988). Naturally, the value of access to an organization varies due to the political situation and the issues involved. Elective uncertainty is also included in PAC calculations, as "some [PACs] are paragons of pragmatism, choosing only incumbents and likely winners as recipients (Sabato 1984, 72)" of their contributions.

Two final, interrelated questions remain concerning PAC strategies: the committee assignment and the voting record of a candidate. Those assigned to committees such as Ways and Means are likely to garner contributions from a variety of sources while representatives on specialized committees are often beneficiaries of largesse from specific groups or political action committees. Defense industry PACs tend to be big contributors to Armed Services Committee members (Gopoian 1984) while Agriculture Committee members can benefit from tobacco industry PAC contributions, and so on. Incumbents, of course, have a voting record which is scrutinized carefully before a contribution decision is made.[6] While some one-issue PACs impose a litmus test of support on one vote, others consider the representative's total level of support (Herndon 1982, Sabato 1984). A representative can reduce the impact of voting wrong on one occasion by an overall strong level of support. Most PAC directors are understanding of a representative who needs to "vote the district" on one issue that runs counter to their legislative goals if she provides an otherwise consistent level of support. Some one-issue PACs, however, consider a wrong vote grounds for opposing an incumbent or at the very least cutting off support.

If the value of access created by a contribution is viewed as a return on an investment, labeled R, the decision faced by PACs can be formally expressed as:

$$C_i = f (R_i, \quad \sigma_1, \quad \sigma_{wi}, \quad \sigma_{si}).$$
$$(+) \quad (-) \quad (-) \quad (-) \qquad\qquad (5.1)$$

The optimal level of contributions to candidate i, C_i, is determined by: R_i, the expected value of access to this candidate; σ_1, the legislative uncertainty, reflecting the question whether legislation of interest to the interest group will arise during a particular term; σ_{wi}, the uncertainty of candidate i winning the election; and σ_{si}, the uncertainty stemming from the unknown degree of support by candidate i for the pertinent legislation.

Positive and negative signs in parentheses reflect the expected impact of each argument on C_i. In other words, optimal campaign contributions, C^*, are positively related to the value of the particular legislation, negatively related to the legislative uncertainty, negatively related to the uncertainty of a particular candidate winning the election, and negatively related to the level of uncertainty about the candidate's ability to further the special interest group's objectives.

It is inherently difficult for an outside observer to measure R. Indeed, the benefits of a particular legislative action may be vague to the people directly concerned, and it is theoretically impossible for a researcher to impute values for others' tastes and preferences. Fortunately the question of concern in this study does not require an explicit value for R. It is sufficient to assume PACs compute or otherwise divine a benefit level for various projects, regulations, and legislation, and operate with that value in mind. Our interest lies not in the content of specific legislation but with the dispersion of campaign contributions across candidates. Only the uncertainty arising from candidate differences concerns us.

Because we are concerned with relative campaign contributions during an election cycle, the legislative uncertainty, σ_1 is also unimportant in this study. The probability that pertinant legislation will arise during a congressional session certainly affects the benefit calculation for PACs, but it does not affect their relative determination of support across candidates. This category of uncertainty is probably a dominant variable in the explanation of differing levels of PAC contributions across elections; for example, in one year a particular PAC may invest more across the board because it knows crucial legislation is likely to be on the calendar. However, it has minimal impact on decisions to give to particular candidates.[7] Isolating the effects of race and sex requires us to have information on the latter decision.

The second source of uncertainty, σ_{wi}, reflects candidates' probability of winning. Chapter 4 explicitly investigates candidates' desire for contributions based on their probability of winning an election. Contrib-

utors are also concerned with a candidate's chances of success. Measures
of a candidate's electoral strength include the incumbency advantage,
previous election results, and in a decade of substantial Republican
presidential victories, party affiliation may reflect a coattail effect.

The third type of uncertainty, σ_{si}, consists of the candidates' varying
levels of support for the interest group's policy agenda. While the
intensity of a candidate's support cannot be measured directly, past voting
records, party affiliation, and constituent demographics may give insight
into their concerns and constraints on voting decisions (Gopoian 1984,
Poole, Romer, and Rosenthal 1987).[8]

AN EMPIRICAL MODEL OF PAC CONTRIBUTIONS

Five different categories of PAC contributions are empirically investigated for each election cycle during the decade of the eighties. These
PAC categories follow divisions established by the Federal Election
Commission in its postelection reports on financial activity. The categories are: PACs of organized labor (named LABOR$), corporate PAC
contributions (CORP$), trade, memberships, and health committees
(TRADE$), PAC contributions from cooperatives (COOP$), and nonaligned (often without parent organizations) ideological PACs (NON-
ALIGN$).

Before the explicit model is presented, two statistical questions need
to be addressed: How should incumbents and nonincumbents be handled?
What problems arise because of the nature of the data? The summary,
Table 5.1, demonstrates that PACs concentrate their contributions on
incumbents. This by itself is not problematic; for example, if incumbents
received more money because of the heralded incumbent advantage, a
dummy variable for candidate status would suffice. However, incumbents
are probably treated differently than nonincumbents in a more funda-
mental sense. Specifically, a particular candidate characteristic may carry
more or less (or different) information because of the candidate's
incumbency.

Party affiliation is a variable carrying information on ideology and for
some districts the probability of being elected, issues that are of interest
to interest groups. When we compare an untested challenger with an
incumbent, the incumbent has a voting record as well as an electoral
history, both of which give better information than does simple party
affiliation. For this incumbent, party affiliation plays a minor role in the
delineation of ideology, but it carries other useful information, such as
potential committee membership and leadership position in the House.

For a challenger, however, the lack of a record and electoral history forces contributors to rely largely on party affiliation for ideological information and even stength before the electorate. So, PAC decisionmakers may view the same characteristic in a different light dependent on candidate status.

The possibility that incumbents and challengers are viewed differently is crucial because the number of black and female candidates is not evenly divided between incumbents, challengers, and open-seat candidates. For this reason incumbents and nonincumbents are divided into two groups and investigated separately, which allows for a full accounting of potential status differences.[9]

The second statistical complication arises because the dependent variable, PAC contributions, is truncated at zero, that is, there are no negative campaign contributions. This is called a censored data set, in this case censored at zero, and linear regression techniques are inappropriate. James Tobin (1958) constructed a regression technique for these types of problems where a likelihood function combines the attributes of a probit model for the zero observations and ordinary least squares for the positive observations. Since the introduction of this approach, several generalizations and estimation methods for "tobit" regression have been proposed. We follow Maddala (1983) in using a Newton-Raphson maximum likelihood procedure.

Tobit estimates allow us to test hypotheses about direction and significance, but due to the nonlinear combination of OLS and probit techniques the estimated coefficients cannot be relied on for discussions about the magnitude of the change. Because we are interested in the magnitude as well as the significance and direction, the estimated coefficients must be transformed into estimated partial derivatives. This transformation is discussed in the next section. In some cases another tack was adopted. Some categories contain PACs, such as AMPAC (the American Medical Association's PAC) in the trade and membership category, that give money to virtually every incumbent, and so tobit estimates are indistinguishable from OLS estimates. The OLS estimates are reported for these categories because of their superior interpretability.

Specifically, in four of the PAC categories, LABOR\$, CORP\$, TRADE\$, and NONALIGN\$, practically all incumbents receive contributions from one or more PACs in the category. Of these four PAC categories the most serious censoring problem applies to labor PACs in 1980 when 13 percent of the incumbents received no labor PAC money. As an average however, the PACs in these four categories gave money to 95 percent of the incumbents. These few zero observations affect the

magnitude of our observation by small amounts, and the significance of
a variable is not changed in any case. Hence, OLS estimates are reported
in these cases.

On the other hand, all PAC categories in the nonincumbent group as
well as cooperative contributions in the incumbent group have several
truncated observations, and OLS estimates differ from the tobit parameters. Therefore in these cases tobit procedures are used, and the
estimates are transformed to yield estimated partial derivatives.

In general, PAC contributions reflect the value of access tempered by
the probability a candidate will win and the degree of expected support.
Hence, campaign contributions are expected to be determined by the
variables in equation (5.2).

PAC$ = f (CQrating, DEMOCRAT, TENURE, LASTVOTE, VOTEGAP,
              (+)   (?)   (+)   (?)   (−)
          OPPONENT$, COMMITTEE, BLACK, FEMALE).
              (+)   (+)   (?)   (?)   (5.2)

The dependent variable in equation (5.2), PAC$, is a mnemonic
standing for each of the five PAC categories. The five regressions to
be estimated have a specific category as the dependent variable, that
is, the first regression will use LABOR$, the second CORP$ and so
on.

The first explanatory variable, CQrating, is a two-year weighted
average of voting records reported in *Congressional Quarterly*. Each
year the AFL-CIO and the Chamber of Commerce of the United States
review legislators' voting records and rate their support of pro-labor or
pro-business legislation on a 1 to 100 scale. Dividing these ratings by
100 gives a 0 to 1 range reflecting the degree of congressional support
provided by each legislator. Viewing these ratings as a ratio of supportive
votes allows them to be used as a gauge of probable support.[10] A legislator
who has supported all labor initiatives in the previous two years can be
expected to have a higher probability of supporting future pro-labor
legislation than will a representative with a dismal labor voting record.
Conversely, many corporate PACs and trade groups look to the ratings
compiled by the U.S. Chamber of Commerce to gauge an incumbent's
attitude toward the business community. These ratings are included in
the LABOR$ and CORP$ equations respectively because these categories
consist of PACs with relatively homogeneous objectives.

The remaining PACs are handled differently. Because these categories
(TRADE$, COOP$, and NONALIGN$) consist of widely divergent

groups with vastly different (and often competing) political objectives, there is no universal voting record reflecting their collective issues. For example, both the National Abortion Rights Action League PAC and the National Right to Life PAC are major players in the nonconnected category. It would be impossible to devise a single measure reflecting their opposing views on abortion, just as it would for other opposing ideological PACs in this category.

The inclusion of voting records raises a question of simultaneity bias. Specifically, it may be true that organized labor PACs are inclined to support legislators with pro-union voting records, but the causality may run in both directions since legislators may be more inclined to support labor legislation if campaign support from labor has been forthcoming. Simultaneous models for LABOR$ and CORP$ were evaluated, but the estimates for the contributions equation were similar to single-equation estimates.[11] The results of single-equation regressions are easier to interpret, and in the interests of simplicity we report the results of single-equation regressions throughout this chapter.

The signs in parentheses below variable names give predicted effects of the explanatory variables. In equation (5.2) the level of contributions a candidate receives from a political action committee is expected to be positively related to the CQrating, which is a pro-labor scale in the LABOR$ equation and a pro-business rating in the CORP$ equation.

For most PAC categories, the DEMOCRAT dummy variable is expected to be positive because it reflects membership in the majority party that dominates committee membership and the legislative agenda. All else equal, a majority member should be preferable to a minority member for an access-seeking political action committee. However, in some cases the ideological dimension of party affiliation may be dominant, and the sign will be negative.

As indicated in chapter 4, TENURE is a reflection of an incumbent's political clout and the probability of winning. For this reason a positive coefficient is predicted. The square of tenure, included in the previous chapter, is omitted here because its estimated coefficients were never significant and it had no discernable effect on the remaining coefficients.

LASTVOTE measures a candidate's percentage of the vote received in the previous election. As indicated in chapter 4, this variable indicates the strength of the candidate (or the strength of the party for challengers). Political action committees that follow an access-seeking strategy will tend to gravitate to candidates who have a high likelihood of success. However, a countervailing force is the candidate's need for funds. Representatives who achieved an easy victory in their last race are more likely than are marginal winners to consider themselves secure in their next race. There is less pressure for them to raise large sums of money, and so PACs are at a bargaining disadvantage. The "price" a secure candidate is willing to pay for support may be very low, and hence contributions drop.

The VOTEGAP variable is a measure of the tightness of the current election. As the candidate decision model presented in chapter 4 demonstrated, a candidate involved in a close election has a greater desire for additional funds, and the political IOU he is willing to offer is more valuable to contributors. This situation increases the confidence of PACs that access will bear fruit. Because VOTEGAP is calculated such that lower values indicate tighter races, a negative sign is expected. Campaign spending by the opponent, OPPONENT$, is similarly affected. As an opponent increases her campaign expenditures, a candidate wants additional money to offset the potential advantage this spending may cause (see chapter 4). Again, this increased desire for money by the candidate puts the PAC in a more favorable bargaining position and increased funding will generally be expected.

Committee chairmanships or other House leadership positions give representatives additional input on issues which in turn makes access to these individuals more valuable. All else equal, a positive coefficient on COMMITTEE is expected as PACs seek to obtain access to influential members of the House.

After PAC contributions to incumbents are explored, nonincumbents' funding is investigated. Naturally, variables pertaining to incumbent service in Congress are omitted. This eliminates TENURE, COMMITTEE, LASTVOTE, and all voting records, but a dummy variable indicating an open-seat race is added. The inclusion of the OPEN dummy variable helps to control for the expected difference in the funding of challengers and open-seat candidates. While neither offers the degree of security concerning ideological position or chance of victory afforded by incumbents, open-seat candidates are a far more likely bet to gain election than are almost all challengers. This yields equation (5.3):

PAC$ = h (DEMOCRAT, VOTEGAP, OPPONENT$, OPEN, BLACK, FEMALE).
    (?)   (–)   (+)   (+)   (?)   (?)
                                                                    (5.3)

Once again, PAC$ stands for one of the five categories under study. The exclusion of a voting history negates any question of simultaneity bias, and single-equation tobit regression will suffice.

WHO GETS PAC DOLLARS?

Results of the incumbent regressions appear in tables 5.2 through 5.6. In general, measures used to reflect the uncertainty faced by PACs had the predicted signs. In other words, PACs appear to increase contributions when the expected return increases (for a given risk) and to reduce contributions when uncertainty rises.

In the labor and corporate PACs regressions, incumbent voting records were used to measure past support of labor or corporate goals. Assuming this also predicts future support, we expected ratings to be positively related to PAC contributions. This proposition was soundly supported as the ratings were positively and significantly related to labor and corporate PAC contributions in all five election cycles.

Party affiliation is also an important explanatory variable as its coefficient was significantly different from zero for every PAC category, although not in every election. As we expected, Democratic incumbents received more money from labor PACs in all five elections, with the party differential ranging from $4,700 in 1980 to $22,000 in 1986. Corporate PACs also supported Democrats in three of the five elections. Apparently, the positive coefficient in the corporate regressions reflects the Democrats' majority party status. In spite of Republican efforts to stress their identification with business interests, most business PACs preferred to support Democratic incumbents who were more likely to control the levers of power in the House than were their Republican counterparts. The organizations in the trade and membership category also considered party affiliation as they reduced their contributions to Democrats by amounts in the range of $7,800 to $10,200. Interestingly, their bias toward Republican candidates may have reflected the overwhelming influence of several large PACs in this category, such as the National Association of Realtors' R-PAC. However, the anti-Democratic stance of PACs in this category waned late in the eighties, and the sign of the coefficient became positive in 1988 even though the coefficient was not statistically significant. Cooperatives' PACs gave significantly larger contributions to Democratic incumbents in all five elections, although the levels were smaller than for the other categories. Finally, PACs with no parent organizations (NONALIGN$) showed mixed partisan signals. Democratic incumbents received between $3,900 and $9,700 more than Republicans did from PACs in this category, except in 1980 when Republicans were the favored candidates, perhaps reflecting the energies of several New-Right PACs to capture control of Congress in that election.

Table 5.2
Labor PAC Contributions to Incumbents: OLS

	1980	1982	1984	1986	1988
AFL	36.138***	47.251***	62.027***	61.323***	80.344***
	(3.573)	(5.604)	(7.373)	(7.189)	(8.914)
DEMOCRAT	4.787**	12.024***	12.778**	22.312***	16.841***
	(2.174)	(4.025)	(5.144)	(4.979)	(6.388)
TENURE	-.090	-.271	-.810***	-1.028***	-1.362***
	(.125)	(.194)	(.211)	(.226)	(.246)
COMMITTEE	3.392	2.560	13.750***	19.335***	12.485**
	(2.495)	(2.054)	(4.907)	(5.404)	(5.446)
LASTVOTE	-15.092***	-3.215	-48.837***	-4.772	-68.579***
	(5.522)	(8.614)	(12.094)	(11.710)	(13.190)
VOTEGAP	-11.872*	-44.063***	-28.536**	-64.492***	-25.768*
	(4.049)	(10.889)	(11.707)	(13.002)	(13.834)
OPSPEND	.0600***	.0186***	.0610***	.0421***	.0129
	(.0062)	(.0057)	(.0087)	(.0093)	(.0098)
BLACK	-7.486*	-7.350	4.139	10.559	4.776
	(4.369)	(5.842)	(6.236)	(6.916)	(7.091)
FEMALE	-.983	-9.532*	3.803	7.555	1.692
	(3.778)	(5.145)	(5.990)	(6.476)	(6.699)
adj. R^2	.58	.53	.62	.57	.58

Standard errors appear in parentheses below the estimated coefficients.
* indicates significance at the .10 α-level, ** at the .05 α-level,
and *** at the .01 α-level.

Time in office, TENURE, was surprisingly unimportant. In all five categories over all elections, the tenure variable was only intermittently significant, and its sign was negative more often than not. A likely explanation for this unexpected result may be that tenure is a poor measure of a political dimension more accurately reflected in other variables. Specifically, tenure was included because time in Congress usually leads to greater power as seniority and political alliances evolve. In this study, however, the impact of tenure is captured in other ways. First, the candidates are divided into incumbents and challengers. One of the more important consequences of tenure is its reflection of incumbency; for example, having two years of tenure is substantially more important than zero tenure. However, the division of candidates

Table 5.3
Corporate PAC Contributions to Incumbents: OLS

	1980	1982	1984	1986	1988
CCUS	47.935*** (9.979)	70.889*** (9.333)	87.409*** (15.816)	55.681*** (13.889)	68.214*** (15.159)
DEMOCRAT	-.301 (4.179)	16.934*** (5.930)	16.747** (7.419)	12.058 (7.721)	24.323*** (9.493)
TENURE	.149 (.243)	.648** (.271)	.430 (.280)	.422 (.341)	.115 (.366)
COMMITTEE	4.226 (4.862)	-1.706 (2.884)	19.804*** (6.509)	34.125*** (8.020)	30.865*** (7.994)
LASTVOTE	2.313 (10.761)	-5.142 (12.126)	-11.684 (16.072)	12.382 (17.391)	-6.589 (19.278)
VOTEGAP	-16.301 (13.798)	-30.962** (15.169)	-19.285 (15.639)	-42.664** (19.457)	-0.910 (20.345)
OPSPEND	.0555*** (.0121)	.0261*** (.0080)	.0398*** (.0116)	.0567*** (.0139)	.0701*** (.0145)
BLACK	2.206 (8.439)	1.745 (8.164)	-7.081 (8.238)	-1.179 (10.479)	-16.299* (9.375)
FEMALE	-5.813 (7.361)	-.176 (7.188)	6.068 (7.988)	-.883 (9.625)	3.289 (9.828)
adj. R²	.17	.25	.20	.19	.17

Standard errors appear in parentheses below the estimated coefficients.
* indicates significance at the .10 α-level, ** at the .05 α-level,
and *** at the .01 α-level.

into challengers and incumbents absorbs this initial impact. Second, as increased tenure raises a representative's seniority, the likelihood of his occupying a position of power grows. In this study, a dummy variable for committee chairs, ranking minority members, and other House leadership positions is included. Hence, tenure is left as a residual measure of congressional power, and that presence is largely unimportant. A representative who has accumulated a great deal of tenure but who does not hold an influential position in Congress may be an ineffective ally for PACs.

The percentage of the vote received in the last election, LASTVOTE, and the absolute value of the vote margin, VOTEGAP, both had estimated

Table 5.4
PAC Contributions to Incumbents by Trade, Membership, and Health Organizations: OLS Estimates

	1980	1982	1984	1986	1988
DEMOCRAT	-7.896***	-10.253***	-9.198***	-2.039	4.286
	(1.519)	(2.332)	(2.366)	(2.989)	(3.361)
TENURE	-.115	-.126	-.299	-.475**	-.665**
	(.122)	(.186)	(.188)	(.220)	(.225)
COMMITTEE	6.487***	1.006	14.648***	27.666***	15.073***
	(2.448)	(1.984)	(4.220)	(5.268)	(5.468)
LASTVOTE	.813	-1.930	-13.210	16.893	-19.065
	(5.420)	(8.310)	(10.410)	(11.393)	(12.723)
VOTEGAP	-4.353	-26.050**	-11.968	-44.877***	-26.312*
	(6.791)	(10.382)	(10.000)	(12.707)	(13.528)
OPSPEND	.0345***	.0230***	.0387***	.0463***	.0396***
	(.0061)	(.0055)	(.0075)	(.0089)	(.0094)
BLACK	-8.302**	-10.875**	-12.014**	-8.035	-15.895**
	(4.139)	(5.472)	(5.209)	(6.666)	(7.149)
FEMALE	-1.527	-6.370	.454	1.220	5.288
	(3.706)	(4.927)	(5.143)	(6.336)	(6.752)
adj. R^2	.19	.21	.21	.22	.13

Standard errors appear in parentheses below the estimated coefficients.
* indicates significance at the .10 α-level, ** at the .05 α-level,
and *** at the .01 α-level.

coefficients that were usually positive, and one or the other or both were usually significantly so. This was the expected result for VOTEGAP, but our prediction for LASTVOTE was uncertain. Apparently, LASTVOTE carries only marginal information on the probability of victory due to the division of incumbents and challengers, but it signals candidate need. The usual explanation is that a candidate who received a scare in the previous election usually mounts a campaign effort larger than average for the next race even though he faces a weaker challenger. As a result there is a greater demand from the candidate for financial support, and contributors may perceive that they are likely to gain enhanced access from their dollars as the candidate courts them.

Practically every category has a positive and significant coefficient on the opponent's campaign expenditures. As our view of the candidate

Table 5.5
PAC Contributions to Incumbents by Cooperatives
Tobit Estimates and Estimated Partials

	1980	1982	1984	1986	1988
DEMOCRAT	.749*	2.569**	1.742**	1.202*	1.851**
	(.441)	(.766)	(.698)	(.703)	(.665)
	.396	1.506	1.189	.809	1.264
TENURE	-.049	-.155*	-.056	-.109*	-.028
	(.036)	(.062)	(.054)	(.053)	(.049)
	-.026	-.091	-.038	-.073	-.019
COMMITTEE	-.172	.615	.893	2.749**	.058
	(.722)	(.653)	(1.255)	(1.246)	(1.094)
	-.091	.360	.610	1.850	.040
LASTVOTE	-1.500	.169	-6.844**	.932	-6.597***
	(1.579)	(2.719)	(3.066)	(2.664)	(2.494)
	-.794	.099	-4.674	.627	-4.504
VOTEGAP	-5.491***	-8.823***	-2.242	-7.932***	-1.797
	(2.012)	(3.401)	(2.931)	(2.977)	(2.652)
	-2.906	-5.171	-1.531	-5.337	-1.227
OPSPEND	.0018	.0011	.0038*	.0010	.0025
	(.0017)	(.0018)	(.0022)	(.0021)	(.0018)
	.0010	.0006	.0026	.0007	.0017
BLACK	-1.226	-4.940***	-2.856**	-1.554	-.976
	(1.246)	(1.922)	(1.370)	(1.553)	(1.391)
	-.649	-2.895	-1.951	-1.046	-.666
FEMALE	-2.133*	-2.793*	-2.014	-1.158	-1.466
	(1.185)	(1.666)	(1.512)	(1.473)	(1.322)
	-1.128	-1.637	-1.376	-.779	-1.001

Three estimates are reported in each cell. The top number is the Tobit estimated coefficient and its standard error is below in parentheses. Below that is an estimated partial derivative calculated while the remaining explanatory variables are held at their mean (see equation [5.5]).
* indicates significance at the .10 α-level, ** at the .05 α-level, and *** at the .01 α-level.

decision process maintains, spending by one candidate engenders spending by the opponent. With the exception of contributions by PACs in the cooperatives category, this increased demand for funds was an important explanatory variable for virtually all elections and all PAC categories.

We now come to the results of central interest to this study. As indicated previously there are a variety of factors that influence PAC contribution

Table 5.6
**PAC Contributions to Incumbents by Nonaligned Special Interest Groups:
OLS Estimates**

	1980	1982	1984	1986	1988
DEMOCRAT	-1.042**	3.967***	5.451***	6.131***	9.721***
	(.343)	(1.114)	(1.167)	(1.428)	(1.557)
TENURE	-.046*	.092	-.126	-.216*	-.329
	(.028)	(.089)	(.090)	(.105)	(.113)
COMMITTEE	-.027	-2.211**	.458**	2.764	2.130
	(.553)	(.948)	(2.088)	(2.516)	(2.532)
LASTVOTE	-2.047*	-4.193	-18.607***	-12.190**	-26.676***
	(1.224)	(3.969)	(5.160)	(5.441)	(5.893)
VOTEGAP	-.511	-23.983***	-7.357	-21.542***	-23.416***
	(1.534)	(4.959)	(4.960)	(6.069)	(6.265)
OPSPEND	.0174***	.0181***	.0414***	.0407***	.0360***
	(.0014)	(.0026)	(.0037)	(.0042)	(.0043)
BLACK	.221	.278	2.064	.728	2.142
	(.935)	(2.614)	(2.584)	(3.183)	(3.311)
FEMALE	-.664	-2.337	.399	-1.808	-2.297
	(.837)	(2.353)	(2.552)	(3.026)	(3.127)
adj. R²	.42	.31	.43	.39	.38

Standard errors appear in parentheses below the estimated coefficients.
* indicates significance at the .10 α-level, ** at the .05 α-level,
and *** at the .01 α-level.

decisions. Unless PAC directors believe blacks and women are unelect-
able or that they would be automatically prejudiced against their groups
because of race and/or gender, political action committees should be
expected to consider factors other than race or sex when making
contribution decisions.

While there are different levels of PAC contributions to black and
female incumbents, the number of cases is small. Most significant
coefficients for black candidates are negative. Specifically, the results
presented here suggest black incumbents received $7,400 less from labor
PACs in 1980, $16,000 less from corporate PACs in 1988, and $2,800
to $4,900 less from cooperatives' PACs (1982 and 1984). The most
consistent racial effect was for PAC contributions from trade, membership, and health organizations that gave significantly lower levels of

contributions to black incumbent candidates in four of the five election cycles in the decade of the 1980s. And the levels were substantial. In 1980, trade PACs gave $8,300 less to black candidates, and by 1988, this disparity had almost doubled. While a variety of forces are at work here, what is evident is that collectively, black incumbents were at an overall disadvantage when it came to garnering PAC dollars in the eighties.

This disadvantage is even more puzzling because during the eighties some black representatives came to occupy leadership positions in the House. PACs that seemed to pursue an access-oriented strategy on the one hand by supporting strong incumbents in leadership roles turned a blind eye to black incumbents. In 1988, for example, Augustus Hawkins (CA 29), the chair of the House Education and Labor Committee was a PACman par excellence as he received 97.8 percent of his $109,450 campaign receipts from political action committees, with slightly over $61,000 coming from labor PACs.[12] Hawkins easily won re-election, rolling up 83 percent of the vote. Les Aspin, the white chair of the Armed Services Committee, received only 43 percent of his war chest from PACs, but that amounted to 265,249 PAC dollars. Aspin also won comfortably, gaining 76 percent of the vote. While the Defense and Education committees may attract different PAC contributors, both are important committees, and the chair of each is an important figure in the House. Perhaps Hawkins could have received more PAC money had he asked; nonetheless, a more than $150,000 discrepancy in PAC funds exists between him and Aspin. Ronald Dellums (CA 8) is the most notable black representative who has not benefited from PAC largesse. Although Dellums fought expensive campaigns in the eighties, raising large sums of money for each race, he received only between 5.5 percent (1982) and 9.1 percent (1980) of his funding from PACs.[13] Other influential black representatives, such as Charles Rangel (NY 16) and William Gray (PA 2) did well enough from PACs in the 1980s, but overall, black incumbents tended to lag behind their white counterparts.

Female incumbents fared much better than did black incumbents. In only three cases did women receive significantly lower levels of funds than did other incumbents. In 1982, labor PACs gave $9,500 less to female incumbents and the 1980 and 1982 contributions by cooperatives' PAC contributions were significantly lower for female candidates. The estimated partial derivatives suggest these shortfalls were $1,100 to $1,500 for women, who in other dimensions displayed campaign characteristics typical of male incumbents.

The tide seemed to be swinging in favor of female congressional candidates in the late seventies and early eighties (Burrell 1985, Uhlaner and Schlozman 1986, Wilhite and Theilmann 1986), and it appears to have continued for the rest of the eighties. Female incumbents in the eighties seem to have belied the fears expressed by the directors of several women's PACs (Kleeman 1983) early in the decade that female candidates were not being treated equally by political action committees. Although female incumbents raised their campaign funds from a wider variety of sources than did Augustus Hawkins in 1988, many obtained 30 to 40 percent of their war chests from political action committees. For example, in 1980 Virginia Smith (NE 3) obtained 37 percent of her $113,009 from PACs, in 1982 Beverly Byron (MD 6) gathered 50 percent from PACs, in 1984 Lindy Boggs (LA 2) garnered 37 percent from PACs, in 1986 Lynn Martin (IL 16) got nearly 40 percent from PACs, and in 1988 Liz Patterson (SC 4) obtained 39 percent of her $974,666 from PACs.

What is evident is that although the size of campaign war chests grew during the decade, PAC spending matched the overall growth for women. Even when female incumbents were at a disadvantage with some PACs (i.e., labor and cooperative PACs in 1982), overall they fared well. Although female representatives did not occupy any major leadership positions in the House in 1988, several received substantial sums from PACs. Without engaging in a case-by-case analysis, it nonetheless appears that much of this PAC spending was driven by the competitiveness of the race. Patterson, for example, was engaged in a tough re-election battle in a marginal district in 1988. PACs did not seem to consider gender as important as other considerations when they made decisions to contribute to women incumbents in the House.

Tobit estimates for nonincumbents appear in tables 5.7–5.11. As in the previous tables, standard errors are in parentheses below the estimates. Unfortunately, tobit estimates are only reliable as tests for the direction of influence and significance of the explanatory variables. The magnitude of the impact of a particular variable is a more complicated issue. Fortunately, an estimate of the partial derivative of PAC contributions with respect to each explanatory variable can be calculated, and these partials can give us insight into the *magnitude* of a variable's impact. Following Maddala (1983), a partial derivative for each variable will be estimated as:

$$\frac{\delta Y}{\delta X_i} = F\left(\frac{\beta' X}{\sigma}\right) \beta_i. \tag{5.4}$$

where β is a vector of the estimated coefficients, X is a vector of the means of the independent variables, σ is the standard error of the regression, and F indicates the cumulative normal distribution function.

Table 5.7
PAC Contributions to Nonincumbents by Organized Labor
Tobit Estimates and Estimated Partial Derivatives

	1980	1982	1984	1986	1988
DEMOCRAT	38.059***	56.395***	75.331***	89.817**	111.118***
	(2.515)	(3.728)	(4.874)	(6.514)	(7.636)
	19.061	28.221	21.146	20.647	22.884
OPEN	11.308***	14.821***	9.455*	23.694***	31.562***
	(2.335)	(3.427)	(5.542)	(6.026)	(7.866)
	5.663	7.417	2.654	5.447	6.500
VOTEGAP	-91.385***	-170.631***	-204.178***	-356.312***	-399.618***
	(11.814)	(19.915)	(27.173)	(33.616)	(42.812)
	-45.768	-85.391	-57.314	-81.909	-82.297
OPSPEND	.0209***	.0261***	.0174*	.0190**	.0385***
	(.0058)	(.0083)	(.0107)	(.0093)	(.0110)
	.0105	.0131	.0049	.0044	.0079
BLACK	17.088***	15.533*	13.903	52.830***	37.649
	(5.653)	(8.299)	(13.903)	(17.872)	(30.493)
	8.558	7.773	3.903	12.144	7.721
FEMALE	4.372	.051	13.940**	-5.770	-5.897
	(3.211)	(5.420)	(5.940)	(9.044)	(9.596)
	2.190	.026	3.913	-1.326	-1.214

Three estimates are reported in each cell. The top number is the Tobit estimated coefficient and its standard error is below in parentheses. Below that is an estimated partial derivative calculated while the remaining explanatory variables are held at their mean (see equation [5.5]).
* .10 indicates significance at the α-level, ** at the .05 α-level, and *** at the .01 α-level.

These estimated partial derivatives are given below the estimated standard errors.

Once again estimated coefficients for the explanatory variables are usually as expected. Candidates competing for open seats and those in close elections received greater levels of contributions as their demand for funds as well as their probabilities of winning increased. The results of the OPEN variable are particularly interesting as they indicate that PACs tended to be generous to candidates for open seats. The relationship is apparent for both PACs pursuing ideological goals and those following an access-oriented strategy. In the first case these candidates gave ideologically oriented PACs a new face in Congress, one that might be inclined to listen to their message. This same argument applied to

Table 5.8
PAC Contributions to Nonincumbents by Corporations
Tobit Estimates and Estimated Partial Derivatives

	1980	1982	1984	1986	1988
DEMOCRAT	-26.143***	-24.236***	-22.263***	-18.868***	-12.920***
	(3.255)	(2.236)	(3.230)	(2.225)	(2.222)
	-13.090	12.121	-9.090	-8.308	-4.599
OPEN	17.885***	18.267***	25.162***	27.319***	26.166***
	(3.750)	(2.373)	(4.280)	(2.488)	(2.910)
	8.955	9.136	10.274	12.029	9.316
VOTEGAP	-167.594***	-121.787***	-170.844***	-126.102***	-133.260***
	(17.803)	(13.402)	(21.036)	(13.100)	(14.945)
	-83.918	60.908	-69.757	-55.525	-47.445
OPSPEND	.0298***	.0105*	.0327***	.0054	.0066*
	(.0090)	(.0057)	(.0080)	(.0037)	(.0039)
	.0149	.0053	.0134	.0024	.0023
BLACK	17.027**	2.248	-7.697	6.085	15.050
	(8.339)	(5.256)	(9.662)	(8.404)	(12.410)
	8.525	1.124	-3.143	2.679	5.358
FEMALE	-2.595	-.649	-.237	-3.811	2.057
	(5.552)	(3.731)	(4.720)	(3.522)	(3.479)
	-1.482	-.325	-.097	-1.678	.732

Three estimates are reported in each cell. The top number is the Tobit estimated coefficient and its standard error is below in parentheses. Below that is an estimated partial derivative calculated while the remaining explanatory variables are held at their mean (see equation [5.5]).
* .10 indicates significance at the α-level, ** at the .05 α-level, and
*** at the .01 α-level.

access-seeking PACs. The results are augmented by those on VOTEGAP, a measure of the closeness of the race. The positive and significant results of the opponents' spending variable is also indicative of the influence that the closeness of the race had on candidate financial efforts. A candidate who had just won a close open-seat race was likely to remember his friends. Conversely, candidates in open-seat races, especially close ones, were those likely to expend maximum effort in fund-raising as in all other aspects of their campaigns.

Party affiliation may still signal an ideological bent to PACs for nonincumbents as it has significant coefficients in several cases. Specifically, in the labor and corporate nonincumbent equations, the Democrat dummy variable probably serves more as a direct ideological measure

Table 5.9
PAC Contributions to Nonincumbents by Trade, Membership, and
Health Organizations
Tobit Estimates and Estimated Partial Derivatives

	1980	1982	1984	1986	1988
DEMOCRAT	-11.344***	-11.130***	-.233	-5.052***	3.523
	(1.770)	(1.408)	(2.047)	(1.749)	(2.312)
	-5.679	-5.565	-.114	-2.574	1.308
OPEN	13.570***	12.317***	18.662***	24.475***	32.891***
	(3.750)	(2.373)	(4.280)	(2.488)	(2.910)
	6.793	6.187	9.095	12.472	12.216
VOTEGAP	-107.493***	-103.650***	-115.313***	-114.537***	-173.697***
	(10.493)	(8.945)	(13.397)	(10.853)	(17.107)
	-53.812	-51.829	-56.201	-73.653	-64.511
OPSPEND	.0171***	.0038	.0119**	.0008	.0059
	(.0050)	(.0037)	(.0052)	(.0008)	(.0043)
	.0086	.0019	.0058	.0004	.0022
BLACK	8.646*	.526	1.658	.309	16.081
	(4.800)	(3.597)	(5.836)	(7.000)	(13.015)
	4.328	.263	.808	.157	5.972
FEMALE	6.406**	-.617	5.816**	-.073	2.130
	(2.849)	(2.439)	(2.976)	(2.894)	(3.721)
	3.207	-.308	2.883	-.037	.791

Three estimates are reported in each cell. The top number is the Tobit estimated
coefficient and its standard error is below in parentheses. Below that is an estimated
partial derivative calculated while the remaining explanatory variables are held at
their mean (see equation [5.5]).
* .10 indicates significance at the α-level, ** at the .05 α-level, and
*** at the .01 α-level.

than it does for the other categories. Running as a Democrat had a large
positive impact on labor contributions in the range of $38,000 to
$111,000, and negative effects on corporate PACs between $12,000 and
$26,000. The generally negative results in the trade and membership
category are a partial indicator of the financial impact of conservative
groups in this category, groups that wished to change the makeup of
Congress, as they also declined to support Democratic incumbents.
Results in the unaffiliated category are not always consistent with those
of incumbents.

The race and sex of nonincumbent candidates appears to be more
important to PACs than was the case for incumbents. With PACs from
five categories contributing to candidates in five elections, more than 30

Table 5.10
PAC Contributions to Nonincumbents by Cooperatives
Tobit Estimates and Estimated Partial Derivatives

	1980	1982	1984	1986	1988
DEMOCRAT	-.419	1.004**	.339	-.126	2.574***
	(.722)	(.460)	(.760)	(.671)	(.718)
	-.209	.502	.102	-.020	.381
OPEN	4.799***	3.384***	3.892***	4.739***	4.372***
	(.793)	(.495)	(.893)	(.759)	(.801)
	2.400	1.692	1.167	.769	.679
VOTEGAP	-21.473***	-15.011***	-26.528***	-24.858***	-30.740***
	(5.036)	(3.081)	(5.622)	(4.510)	(5.665)
	-10.739	-7.504	-7.958	4.032	-4.555
OPSPEND	-.0001	.0016	.0001	.0001	.0005
	(.0020)	(.0011)	(.0018)	(.0012)	(.0012)
	.00005	.0008	.0000	.0000	.0001
BLACK	1.298	-.365	-1.095	2.131	2.113
	(2.268)	(1.437)	(2.725)	(2.048)	(3.126)
	.649	-.182	-.328	.346	.313
FEMALE	.111	-.306	1.967**	-1.057	-3.097**
	(1.217)	(.779)	(1.008)	(1.248)	(1.485)
	.055	-.153	.590	-.171	-.459

Three estimates are reported in each cell. The top number is the Tobit estimated coefficient and its standard error is below in parentheses. Below that is an estimated partial derivative calculated while the remaining explanatory variables are held at their mean (see equation [5.5]).
* .10 indicates significance at the α-level, ** at the .05 α-level, and
*** at the .01 α-level.

percent of their contribution decisions were significantly affected by the race or sex of the candidate. Patterns for contributions to blacks are largely opposite and more pronounced for nonincumbent blacks than for incumbent blacks. For example, the coefficients on race in the labor PAC model are positive in all five years and significantly so in three of the five elections. The estimated partial derivatives suggest nonincumbent blacks received from $6,000 to $25,000 more than comparable white candidates did from labor PACs.

While the coefficients on corporate PAC contributions to black incumbents were usually negative (significantly so in a single case), they are usually positive in the nonincumbent results. Indeed, the sole significant coefficient is positive, suggesting an increase in corporate contributions

Table 5.11
PAC Contributions to Nonincumbents by Nonaligned Special Interest Groups
Tobit Estimates and Estimated Partial Derivatives

	1980	1982	1984	1986	1988
DEMOCRAT	-7.300***	-4.185***	-2.428	-.334	7.160***
	(1.171)	(1.291)	(1.752)	(1.915)	(2.219)
	-3.652	-2.094	-1.349	-.192	3.171
OPEN	4.138***	3.316**	6.710***	13.812***	16.162***
	(1.328)	(1.449)	(2.465)	(2.298)	(3.098)
	2.070	1.659	3.728	7.947	7.157
VOTEGAP	-77.413***	-82.556***	-130.738***	-148.821***	-156.957***
	(6.991)	(7.833)	(11.818)	(11.811)	(15.013)
	-38.727	-41.316	-72.644	-85.821	-69.505
OPSPEND	.0184***	.0193***	.0228***	.0110***	.0237***
	(.0031)	(.0035)	(.0045)	(.0033)	(.0040)
	.0092	.0096	.0127	.0063	.0105
BLACK	3.275	4.736	2.230	33.167***	33.141**
	(3.559)	(3.148)	(4.987)	(7.824)	(13.279)
	1.638	2.370	1.239	19.083	14.676
FEMALE	4.763***	6.024***	6.418***	3.222	8.233**
	(1.820)	(3.148)	(2.544)	(3.068)	(3.584)
	2.383	3.015	3.566	1.854	3.646

Three estimates are reported in each cell. The top number is the Tobit estimated coefficient and its standard error is below in parentheses. Below that is an estimated partial derivative calculated while the remaining explanatory variables are held at their mean (see equation [5.5]).
* .10 indicates significance at the α-level, ** at the .05 α-level, and
*** at the .01 α-level.

to nonincumbent blacks of $8,000 in 1980. Finally, nonaligned PACs appeared to favor black candidates slightly because all five coefficients are positive, two significantly so, and a third is significant with a broader 85 percent confidence interval.[14]

Examination of PAC funding for some individual black challengers and open-seat candidates helps to bear out the regression results. In 1980, for example, Mervyn Dymally (CA 31) defeated the incumbent Charles Wilson in the Democratic primary and went on to win an easy victory in November. Although Dymally received only 15.5 percent ($74,228) of his $479,647 from PACs, it was spread between labor (58.7 percent), corporate (14.2 percent), and trade and membership (14.3 percent) sources. George Crockett's (who also won an open seat that year) funding was more typical as he garnered 26.5 percent ($15,550) of his receipts from PACs, but 86.2 percent of that came from labor PACs. In 1982, the Republican party provided substantial financial support (16.6 percent of total funding) to John Conway, the black challenger to Gerry Studds (MA 10). This party support may have led trade and membership PACs to contribute 66.8 percent of Conway's $27,623 in PAC receipts. Although PACs generally did not support Ron Dellums (CA 8), they did aid substantially his black Republican challenger in 1984. Although Charles Connor only received $38,100 (20.8 percent of the total) to Dellums's $76,752 (8.1 percent of the total) in PAC funds, he outdrew Dellums from corporate, trade and membership, and nonaligned PACs. Dellums, however, raised $58,468 from labor PACs, while Connor obtained no labor money. Michael Lesage, the Democratic challenger to Bill Thomas (CA 20) raised only $23,703 in his lopsided loss in 1984, with only $1,000 coming from PACs, half of that from labor PACs. In 1986, PACs supported Faye Williams's bid to gain the vacancy left by Cathy Long's retirement from the Louisiana Eighth District seat. Williams received $151,129 (37.1 percent of the total) from PACs, but lost a close race to Clyde Holloway. Williams blamed her defeat on her race (the district has a 38 percent black population) and sex, and hoped by familiarity to overcome these drawbacks in 1988 when she challenged Holloway (Duncan 1989, 629). She drew 30.9 percent of her campaign treasury of $493,951 from PACs, but was outspent by Holloway and lost by a wider margin than she did in 1986. Mike Espy, on the other hand, mounted a successful challenge to Webb Franklin (MS 2) in 1986 in a district comprising the Mississippi Delta, which had a majority black population (Duncan 1989, 828). Espy raised funds easily, gaining $296,892 of his $600,375 total from PACs. Two years later, running as an incumbent, Espy handily defeated his Republican challenger, raising $470,960 (53.5 percent of the total) from PACs in all categories. While these individual cases are not always consistent with the regression results, they nonetheless convey a perception that some black non-incumbent candidates are doing well from PACs.

Female nonincumbent candidates were significantly helped by labor PACs in 1984 and by trade, membership, and health PACs in 1980 and 1984. Cooperatives' PACs danced back and forth with significantly greater contributions in one year but significantly lower contributions in another. Both of these years involve relatively small sums. The strongest PAC signal for female candidates was from the nonaligned ideological PACs. All five election years had positive coefficients, and in four of those years they were significantly positive. Overall, the PACs of this category contributed between $2,000 and $6,000 more to female non-incumbents than to their male counterparts. This category includes two groups supportive of female candidates, the National Organization of Women's Campaign Fund and the National Women's Political Caucus Victory Fund–PAC, but neither commanded resources comparable to those of AMPAC or some union political action committees.

As was the case for incumbents, some female challengers and open-seat candidates did well with PACs. Others, running in lopsided races, were ignored. In 1980, the Democratic party activist Polly Baca Barragan ran for an open seat created by Jim Johnson's (CO 4) retirement. She raised 30 percent of her $116,938 war chest from political action committees, particularly labor PACs, but was decisively defeated. Nancy Johnson (CT 6) was more successful in her run for an open seat in 1982, drawing 35 percent of her campaign funds from PACs in the process. Conversely, Nancy Pryor obtained only $718 (out of a total of $12,950) in PAC money in her quixotic quest to defeat Austin Murphy (PA 22) in 1984. Running for an open seat in 1986, Liz Patterson (SC 4), a member of the South Carolina legislature, obtained $156,532 (25.3 percent of the total) from PACs, but when she ran for re-election two years later she more than doubled her PAC receipts, which then made up 39 percent of her war chest.[15] As is the case for male candidates, women fared better with political action committees when they ran as incumbents than when they ran as challengers or open-seat candidates.

In summary, political action committees appear at times to base their contribution decisions on a candidate's race or gender, but the degree of their response to these characteristics depends on the status of the candidate. There is a much larger impact on contributions to challengers than on those to incumbents, and the differentiation is greater for black candidates than for female candidates. Finally, the direction of impact is also incumbent-specific. In general, the significant racial and sexual biases in the incumbent categories were negative, while they were usually positive for the nonincumbent group.

From the perspective of increasing the number of blacks and women in Congress, there is good news and bad news here. First, the tendency of at least some types of PACs to support nonincumbent blacks and women is encouraging. Without substantial institutional support such candidates have little chance of success. Unfortunately, the strength of the OPEN variable indicates that PAC support is likely to lie with candidates for open seats, not with challengers. Because most women run as challengers, this dims their hopes. The same can be said for black candidates who also may have to overcome the challenge of running in a majority-white district.

NOTES

1. The term *interest group* is used here to represent all sorts of interest groups, such as labor-union members, corporations, groups of professionals such as doctors, and simply like-minded citizens. Some interest groups, especially some corporations, may decline to organize a political action committee, preferring to rely on lobbying (see Sorauf 1984, Masters and Keim 1985, Eismeier and Pollock 1985). Nonetheless, the use of a PAC as an aid to lobbying became increasingly common in the eighties. The growth of leadership PACs, political action committees organized by a member of Congress or a presidential candidate, is a relatively new phenomenon, but they are still designed to gain support for the views of the organizer (often by gaining support for his candidacy for office).

2. Even if the only political outlet for a particular objective is national politics, participants of a group have many competing concerns. For example, attention given to family and career absorbs energy and resources, and these concerns compete with the members' political interests.

3. The question of individual motivation and the benefits flowing from interest group membership is a thorny one. Mancur Olson (1965) questions the logic of individual participation to achieve group goals, emphasizing the tendency of group members to become free riders. Russell Hardin (1982), in particular, argues for a logic of individual action to achieve group goals. Terry Moe (1980) emphasizes that Olson neglects political goals in considering group membership. We do not propose to enter into this debate here, concentrating our attention on PAC decisions to contribute to candidates.

4. Naturally there is a marketing gain; a group may want an issue in the spotlight during the election, and even a loss will yield some benefit. In fact this publicity may actually be the short-term goal of an interest group. Some PACs even go as far as to support challengers to well-entrenched incumbents, knowing the chance of victory is slim. In this case they are sending a message to the incumbent that further opposition will follow, or in some cases they may be using their efforts as a ploy to raise additional contributions. In this situation, the target of the group is publicity.

5. There is an extreme case that involves a candidate who lies, promising one thing and delivering another; a decidedly short-term and hence rare strategy. The scenario more commonly involves a representative who passively supports certain legislation, voting in the affirmative when the opportunity arises, as opposed to the vigorous champion who pushes legislation to the floor and encourages others' support.

6. PACs often scrutinize for ideological clues the voting records of state legislators who run for Congress.

7. The empirical question of why the level of PAC activity differs from election year to election year is certainly one of interest. One reason may be the different expectations about legislative uncertainty. Another is that some campaign money is channeled off into presidential campaigns every four years.

8. On some occasions PACs also base their decisions on the identity of the opponent. For example, a challenger taking on an incumbent with a record of opposition to organized labor is more likely to benefit from labor PAC dollars than is

a challenger in another district; and other groups, such as the National Rifle Association, which has supported candidates running against gun control advocates (Sabato 1984) also seem willing to accept the uncertainty of a challenger to the certainty of a known opponent.

9. PACs may treat challengers and open-seat candidates differently for other reasons, but at least on ideological grounds they are both equally lacking in a record (unless they have held office before), setting them off from incumbents. One way to allow for complete flexibility between incumbents and challengers is to run a single equation with an dummy variable for candidate status and interaction terms between this dummy and all the other exogenous variables. While the interaction approach is mathematically identical to our approach, it is less conducive to interpretation.

10. The use of interest-group ratings as a measure of representatives' ideology has been questioned by Richard Carson and Joe Oppenheimer (1984), but for economic interest groups these ratings have a good deal of reliability.

11. The two-equation model added a voting probability equation as in (5.2a):

$$AFL = g \ (LABOR\$, \ DEMOCRAT, \ \%UNION, \ RTW, \ RPV). \qquad (5.2a)$$

where %UNION measures the percentage of constituents belonging to unions, RTW is a dummy variable for states with right-to-work laws, and RPV is the district vote for the Republican presidential candidate in the most recent election. For the CORP\$ model, AFL is replaced with the Chamber of Commerce ratings (CCUS). Because the AFL and CCUS rating are a value lying between zero and one, standard statistical techniques are once again inappropriate. In this case a logit model is required leading to a logit-tobit model for the system. The variables in this equation behave as expected with positive signs on the first two variables and negative signs on the remainder. Particularly interesting was the positive and significant relationship of money on votes in all years, which agrees with the bulk of the most recent voting literature (Wilhite and Theilmann 1987, Wilhite and Paul 1989). More importantly, the simultaneity bias has a larger effect with the estimates of (5.2a) being more sensitive to the model employed. This simultaneity bias is relevant for studies of congressional voting but less important for money studies such as ours.

12. In 1982 Carl Perkins (KY 7), Hawkins's predecessor as chair of the Education and Labor Committee, received 92 percent of his campaign chest from PACs, especially from organized labor.

13. Dellums received 8.1 percent of his campaign dollars from PACs in 1984, 6.9 percent in 1986, and 7.7 percent in 1988, which was $88,445 of his total of $1,153,750.

14. The coefficients on black nonincumbents in 1986 should be viewed with care because there are only two blacks in that category.

15. Louise Slaughter raised even more than Patterson did in 1986 when she challenged and easily defeated Fred Eckert (NY 30). She received $273,431 in PAC money (46.5 percent of her total) in 1986. Slaughter had considered a run for the open seat in 1984, but decided to remain in the New York legislature (Fowler and McClure 1989). When she ran as an incumbent in 1988, Slaughter upped her PAC total to $388,490, which was 49.8 percent of her total campaign funds.

Chapter Six

Party Money: An Affirmative Action Stance?

The campaign finance reforms of the early seventies limited political parties' ability to raise money and channel it to their candidates, forcing them to redefine their role. But to conclude parties are ineffective and/or that most candidates have little interest in party support would be inappropriate. Party support still contributes significantly to candidates' success. Comparing party contributions to all PAC money or to all individual contributions is misleading. A political party has a great deal of control over contributions and spending, while total PAC funds and individual contributions come from many sources with a variety of interests. A more accurate assessment of a party's financial role would be to compare total party contributions with contributions from a single PAC or a single individual or, at best, a closely coordinated group of PACs or individuals. Viewed in this light, political party contributions are one of the larger sources of funds.

The McGovern presidential campaign of 1972 pioneered a new style of party fund-raising, direct mail, but the Republican party first capitalized on its vast potential. During the seventies the Republican National Committee (RNC) modernized its operations, developing a sophisticated fund-raising capability. From this base, Republican strategists provided polling and targeting information to Republican congressional candidates in addition to advice on advertising and organization. By the early eighties the RNC and the National Republican Congressional Committee were able to provide substantial help to many Republican congressional candidates. This help enabled Republican candidates to present a better image, enhancing their ability to secure contributions from other sources.

By 1982, Republican campaign contributions were substantial and well allocated (Jacobson 1985–86), enabling Republican candidates to overcome partially the expected midterm falloff in seats.

Long burdened by campaign debts, the Democratic National Committee (DNC) lagged far behind the Republican party in sophistication and fund-raising throughout the seventies. Gradually they began to regain lost ground. Aggressive leadership by Representative Tony Coelho, who headed the Democratic Congressional Campaign Committee in the early eighties, pioneered a way to financial solvency for the Democrats.

Although the Republican party continued to enjoy a funding advantage in the latter half of the eighties, Democrats were gaining ground. Both parties were becoming increasingly sophisticated in the assistance they offered congressional candidates. Party money is no longer as dominant as it was in the nineteenth century, but it still has an important role in congressional campaigns. PACs often take a lack of party support for challengers or open-seat candidates as an indication that a campaign is hopeless, and so few PACs support challengers and open-seat candidates who cannot obtain the support of their own parties. Conversely, early party support, especially when coupled to aid with PAC solicitation, can enable challengers to become creditable or maintain incumbents in office in the face of stiff challenges.

While nonfinancial party support in areas such as fund-raising or other forms of campaign advice is becoming increasingly important (Herrnson 1988), such support is difficult to measure accurately. Financial assistance can, however, be measured and is a useful proxy for overall party support.

The Democratic and the Republican parties give financial assistance to candidates in two ways: contributions, which are self-explanatory, and coordinated party spending, which consists of expenditures by party committees on behalf of candidates. While these funds have been increasing throughout the 1980s, their rate of growth is just keeping pace with other sources of contributions, and the proportion of all contributions composed of party money remains stable.

In general, the Republican party channels more money to its candidates than does the Democratic party, although the difference in average contributions is declining. Also, the composition of party money appears to be changing. In the 1980s, the share of aggregate party money consisting of national party contributions has dropped relative to national party expenditures. At the beginning of the decade, 65 percent of the parties' funds were contributions to candidates, with 35 percent being expenditures on behalf of candidates. By the 1988 election, the proportions had flip-flopped, with expenditures making up 65 percent of the pie.

Dating from the 1970s, political scientists have become concerned with what is termed the decline of American political parties.[1] Other commentators argue that the parties are alive and well (e.g., Schlesinger 1985, Kayden and Mahe 1985, Herrnson 1988). What is certainly evident is that the Republican and Democratic parties of the 1980s are quite different from the parties of the 1950s. Party loyalty is down; voters no longer vote straight tickets with regularity, and candidates often run their own campaigns independent of the party machinery. The partisan allegiance of the electorate in the 1980s was a fickle one, centered on candidates and issues, not the parties. At the beginning of the decade many candidates turned away from the parties to run independent campaigns, campaigns that were implicitly critical of the congressional parties at times.

Nonetheless, parties are adjusting to their evolving political role, and their influence on national elections remains strong. Party leaders no longer name congressional candidates, and most observers view this as a positive step. In the eighties, Democratic and Republican campaign committees became purveyors of money, fund-raising assistance, and technical campaign advice. Party committees directed these products to specific candidates, but some aid, such as advertisements to "vote Republican for a change," benefited party candidates across the board.

In addition to their changing campaign role, another aspect of party organization in the seventies and eighties concerns us: the reception of blacks and women by the Democratic and Republican parties. The Democrats took the first steps toward broadening participation in party decision making with the McGovern-Fraser Commission, appointed shortly after the 1968 elections. This group, chaired first by Senator George McGovern and then by Congressman Donald Fraser after McGovern resigned to run for president, broadened popular control of the party. One means was the adoption of a quota system to ensure that women and blacks would be adequately represented as delegates to presidential nominating conventions. In essence, affirmative action had come to the Democratic National Convention, and state parties which had to adopt the national reforms. While the reforms of the McGovern-Fraser Commission did not immediately open the door for more women and blacks to run for Congress, they did indicate a commitment by the party to include them in the decision-making process. Republican reforms of the 1970s were less wideranging than were Democratic reforms, partially because Republicans continued to regard the national party as an agent of the state parties and imposed no top-down changes. Nonetheless, the Republican party created a reform commission in the early seventies, a body that worked to open the presidential nominating process to minorities. Both parties finished the seventies making public commitments to blacks and women, commitments that were not always fulfilled by assistance when blacks or women ran for office.

In the eighties, both parties tried to woo black and female voters. The Democrats emphasized their support of affirmative action and often capitalized on a working alliance with women's groups such as the National Organization of Women. The Republicans tried to capitalize on the growth of a black middle class and appealed to women of conservative backgrounds. Each party organized special women's and blacks' committees as part of their efforts. Both parties seemed to put more attention into attracting female congressional candidates than they did in supporting black congressional candidates. This attention took a variety of forms, but one was the provision of campaign resources for the candidates.

A MODEL OF PARTY CONTRIBUTION DECISIONS

Our interest lies in the contribution decisions of political parties. What are the concerns of political parties and how do these concerns affect their contribution decisions? Is there a statistically discernable racial or sexual dimension to this choice? This chapter follows the now-familiar approach. First, a theoretical model of contribution decisions by political parties is derived, then an empirical section provides a test of the usefulness of that theory. Race and gender measures are included to test for discrimination.

An oft-quoted definition of a political party is, "a team seeking to control the governing apparatus by gaining office in a duly constituted election (Downs 1957, 25)." From this perspective, winning is paramount, and ideology is merely a tool used to obtain this objective. Succinctly stated once again by Downs, "parties formulate policies in order to win elections rather than win elections in order to formulate policies (1957, 28)." Using this approach, Joseph Schlesinger argues that because more congressional elections are being contested today than ever before, "the major parties have never been healthier (1984, 396)."

This elegant Downsian thesis has resurfaced in spatial theories encompassing participation and voting (Aldrich 1983a, 1983b, Enlow and Hinich 1984), and it has been broadened by efforts to distinguish between vote maximizing and plurality maximization (Hinich and Ordeshook 1970). Still, there is a constant that binds these theories together—the primary goal of parties is to win elections.

Meanwhile, empirical studies find important ideological components in party affiliation. Poole and Daniels (1985) claim 80 percent of the variation in legislative voting is explained by a single liberal-conservative dimension. Similarly, William Shaffer (1982) shows a consistent ideological split along party lines. Earlier works (Turner and Schneier 1970, Clausen 1973, Clausen and Van Horn 1977) lend support to the contention that ideology and party affiliation have had a stable relationship over a long period of time.

Initially there appears to be an inconsistency in this ideological motivation argument. If parties adopt a platform with the sole objective of winning, then a historical party ideology would be merely coincidental. The long-term stability of a party's ideology found in the empirical studies casts doubt on this explanation. Viewed from the opposite side, if a party exists because of ideology and if it adheres to this ideology, it will consistently lose to a party adopting a winning strategy. This apparent dilemma has led researchers to try to reconcile theory and empirical results.

Kenneth Shepsle (1972) offered one potential explanation by introducing risk. He suggested voters resist the unknown (they are risk-averse), and so the adoption of an identifiable platform can be beneficial. This lends inertia to a party's ideology once it is learned by the electorate.

In another approach, Schlesinger (1975) suggested that there are two types of party members: office seekers and benefit seekers. The former want to gain power, and ideology takes a back seat as suggested by Downs. The second type of individual views the office as a means to an end (the collection of certain benefits). Benefit seekers want parties to adopt an ideology and for allegiances to be known. Schlesinger (1975) suggested both types of individuals exist in all parties, resulting in a combination strategy that stresses winning and ideology.[2]

Other studies assume both ideology and winning are party objectives (Chappell and Keech 1986, Wittman 1973), and then explore the implications of these assumptions. These works, however, do not ask why ideology matters, but just adopt it as a working premise to be tested empirically. In this chapter a reconciliation of the apparent importance of both winning and ideology is offered, one that does not rely on the specific preferences of voters or candidates (as do Shepsle and Schlesinger).

Our thesis suggests the importance of ideology to be office-specific, so strategies for congressional seats differ from strategies for executive campaigns. The theoretical works discussed above seem to be particularly applicable to executive-office elections. Simply stated, when a candidate runs for the presidency or a governorship, the state hands over the prize to the winner and she gains leadership of that branch of government. The degree of control has institutional constraints, but winning is the key. The primary problem for parties after an election is to distribute the benefits of victory (or the costs of defeat).

Controlling the legislative branch is different. First, a majority (or some workable coalition) must be established. Even then, control is not guaranteed because representatives may not support each other's legislation. In other words, to control the governing apparatus a party must encourage its members to cooperate after the election is over. The need for a coherent majority after the election creates a need for party unity that, in turn, leads to an identifiable ideology.[3]

While an identifiable ideology is beneficial to a party, the nature of that ideology is unimportant. For a party to govern it does not matter whether it is liberal or conservative as long as most of its members agree on certain principles. Therefore, the ideological stance of a party is probably affected by the desire to win the election. Still, the necessity of a cohesive majority in a legislature after the election requires unified support of the selected strategy.

Achieving party unity in the House of Representatives has always been a difficult task and has become more so in the eighties. Through the early seventies committees and particularly committee chairs dominated congressional government (Fenno 1973). The power of the Speaker was weak relative to the power of the chairs, who were able to thwart reform efforts. Starting in the late sixties and further evolving in the early seventies, reform efforts broke the old power of chairs but did not centralize power in the hands of the congressional party leadership. Instead, a fragmentation of power occurred in the House as the reformers, on balance, weakened the power of the parties in government (Smith and Deering 1984, Waldman 1980). In such a situation the leadership of both parties had difficulty enforcing party discipline; members felt free to pursue their own agenda, voting with the party when it served their interests. Yet, by the 100th Congress (1987–88) the Democratic leadership had reasserted itself (Sinclair 1990) and made a stronger effort to maintain party discipline.

Since structural reforms of Congress in the early seventies and campaign financial reforms of the same era, leaders of the congressional parties have had a variety of ways of maintaining party unity in the House. The party that controls the White House obviously has presidential favors to distribute; unfortunately for the Republicans they have been in a minority in the House even though they controlled the presidency in the eighties. Nonetheless, through presidential favors and with a large campaign treasury, Republican congressional leaders were in a position to encourage waverers, reward supporters, and discourage backsliders. The Democratic leadership operated in a framework of wide member autonomy, but it too by the end of the eighties was developing a large campaign war chest. Controlling the House machinery, Democrats would reward loyalists through such means as office assignments and committee assignments (the Republicans also use this latter tactic). For example, Jim Chapman received a prized seat on the Appropriations Committee in late 1988 as a reward for casting a politically difficult vote that enabled the Democratic leadership to push through part of its program (Sinclair 1990, 232).

A party's ideology can change over time, but dramatic change is unsettling and so a great deal of inertia exists, inertia that often drives both parties toward the ideological center. This situation is especially true for a party that has a continuing majority. A majority party simply needs to instill discipline within its ranks in order to prevail. Known alliances and objectives will be adopted by this party because innovative ideas may not carry a majority. A minority party has less to loose. Unity within its ranks does not lead to control (unless there is dissention within the majority party) and so new policies and strategies can be forwarded, discussed, and tested in the electoral arena to see if a new majority can be constructed.[4]

From this perspective, a party has two theoretical goals during congressional campaigns. It wants to win seats in the House and it wants to encourage party loyalty. Generalizing the vote optimizing model introduced by John Dobra and William Eubank (1985) and expanded by Wilhite (1988) and Wilhite and Theilmann (1989), this decision can be expressed formally in equation (6.1).

$$S^* = p(T) + r\sigma + C. \tag{6.1}$$

Assume a party identifies the proportion of seats in the legislative body, $p(T)$, required to achieve its objectives: p is the fraction of seats desired and T is the total number of seats available ($T = 435$ in this work). An optimal campaign strategy entails targeting S^* seats during the campaign. S^* is greater than or equal to the desired number of seats, $p(T)$, because of uncertainty in elections, σ, the party's aversion to this risk, r, and the expected number of net crossover votes, C.

For a party primarily concerned with obtaining a simple majority, p is equal to one-half, suggesting the marginal importance of additional seats declines steeply after the majority is attained. A system in which a two-thirds majority (i.e., veto-proof) is required for most legislation will have a larger p. Naturally, p could be a function allowing more-complicated relationships such as increasing returns until a particular proportion is attained and then level or declining returns after that point, but the simple formulation in which $p = 1/2$ will be sufficient for our purposes.

First-order partial derivatives of equation (6.1) ($\delta S/\delta r$, $\delta S/\delta \sigma$, $\delta S/\delta C$) are all assumed to be positive. As a party's risk aversion to an uncertain outcome (r) rises, as the uncertainty of this outcome (σ) increases, and as the expected number of crossover votes (C) rises, the optimum number of seats (S*) increases.

This objective function leads to a two-pronged strategy for political parties. As a campaign progresses, parties can pour their resources into close races in the hopes of winning additional seats. This should lower the uncertainty of seat totals (σ) and/or increase the party's confidence (lower r). Lopsided contests should be ignored because the darkest horses are a waste of money while sure winners do not need help. At the same time, the party can try to fortify unity by helping loyal members. So, to obtain their target number of seats, S*, parties can increase their chances of additional victories, or they can increase loyalty and reduce the number of crossovers.

MEASURING PARTY CONTRIBUTIONS

Political parties have a variety of tools available for use in elections. They provide money, expertise, and polling information; they can tap a network of national, state, and local party organizations; and they may encourage party leaders to visit a candidate's district. All of this activity is brought to bear during congressional elections with the goal of obtaining a loyal majority in the House.

Unfortunately it is difficult to define a unit of measure for many of these services. For example, how much is it worth to a congressional candidate for the vice-president to visit his district and generate some favorable news coverage? While many important party activities are unmeasurable, the amount of money contributed directly or indirectly to a campaign by the party acts as a suitable proxy for this broad-based party support. As a party makes a greater financial commitment to a candidate, it generally supplies other resources as well. If a party does not support a candidate, she gets little financial or "in-kind" assistance. The empirical section of this chapter provides a measure of the relative importance several candidate characteristics have on party considerations and ultimately the parties' ability to win seats and to cajole their members to support a coherent ideology.

Given the scarce resources available to parties, they are expected to target close races because these campaigns are most likely to gain (or lose) seats.[5] Such activity reflects a preoccupation with a strategy of winning seats. In addition, parties may provide greater assistance to candidates who are more likely to support the party position once elected. This second possibility arises from the need to obtain a legislative majority after the election. In an era of boll weevil Democrats and gypsy moth Republicans, party affiliation is no guarantee of support for the goals of the party's congressional leadership. Simply winning seats is not enough to ensure that party legislative goals will be achieved.

A third potential goal motivating party contribution decisions is implicit support for affirmative action—specifically the election of blacks and women to Congress and their continuation in office once they get to Washington. This goal may come less from altruism and more from a desire to attract new voters to the party standard. While this goal is expected to be distinctly subservient to the other two, if the two major parties are commited to increased representation for women and blacks, are they willing to let their money do their talking?

Following this philosophy, campaign contributions made by political parties, called PARTY$, should be determined by party unity, tight-race measures (the party's desire to win seats in Congress), and gender- and race-related characteristics. Specific relationships to be estimated empirically are given in equation (6.2).

PARTY$ = f (PU, OPEN, LASTVOTE, VOTEGAP, OPPONENT$, BLACK,

      (+)   (+)   (+,-)   (-)   (+)   (?)

      FEMALE).

      (?)   (6.2)

If winning a majority is the party's primary goal, a candidate's loyalty is immaterial, but if the party wants to pass legislation, loyalty becomes important. For this reason a measure of expected party support is constructed and included in equation (6.2). *Congressional Quarterly* calculates a party unity index for each session (hereafter called PU) for each member of the House. This index reflects how often a representative votes with his party. Specific votes include issues in which a majority of one party opposes a majority of the other party.

If parties are primarily concerned with winning seats in Congress or if they are uncertain about their ability to obtain (or maintain) their targeted number of seats, they will pump money into close races in which they have a chance to pick up (or not lose) a seat (Jacobson 1985–86). Four variables, OPEN, LASTVOTE, VOTEGAP, and OPPONENT$, are used to capture various aspects of a candidate's probability of winning an election. If winning is the primary strategy, these variables should explain most of the variation in party contributions.

The dummy variable (OPEN), which is set equal to 1 for open-seat races, is expected to have a positive coefficient because open-seat races usually attract strong candidates who spend large amounts of money. The absence of an incumbent raises the possibility that a party can gain (or lose) a seat in the House. Hence, both parties are expected to target these races for the expenditure of their resources.

LASTVOTE, the percentage of the previous election's vote, is expected to be positive for incumbents as a strong showing in the previous race is evidence of a "safe" congressional seat. If an incumbent wins by an unexpectedly close margin, both parties see an opportunity. The incumbent probably redoubles her effort to ward off defeat in the next election, and a challenger's party sees an opportunity to pick up a seat. Therefore, LASTVOTE is expected to be positively related to party contributions for nonincumbents, but negatively related for incumbents.

VOTEGAP again measures the closeness of the current election. To the extent election results are anticipated through polls, a small votegap suggests that the race was tight in the closing days if not throughout the entire campaign. Because close races generate additional spending by both parties, its coefficient is expected to be negative.

Throughout our discussion an increase in spending by one candidate has been expected to generate additional spending by the opponent. This is no exception. Opposition expenditures (OPPONENT$) are predicted to be positively related to campaign spending.

The remaining dummy variables reflect the race and sex of the candidates. If political parties make contribution decisions based on ideology and the probability of winning, there is little reason to expect a racial or gender difference. If, however, a goal is expanding the representation of blacks and women, party money should flow to such candidates, especially if they are viable challengers or open-seat candidates. Hopeless female and black candidates can expect little in the way of party resources.

Financial data applying to the Republican and Democratic parties are divided into four categories before the estimation proceeds. First, incumbents and nonincumbents are separated because the expected impact of some variables differs depending on candidate status. Party unity, PU, drops out of the nonincumbent equations because these candidates generally have no record on which party officials can base a judgment. The second division is along party lines. Separating Democrats and Republicans allows us to observe differences between the parties. Party unity, for example, might be more important to one party, while the previous election results might have more of an impact for the other. These differences would reflect differing election strategies by the parties. This division enables us to question the impact of the candidate's race and gender on party contribution decisions, including whether the two parties treat black/female candidates differently than party campaign committees treat their white/male counterparts.

WHO GETS PARTY CONTRIBUTIONS?

Results of the incumbent regressions appear in tables 6.1 and 6.2, and nonincumbent estimates are in tables 6.3 and 6.4. These equations are estimated with three different dependent variables. The first dependent variable, party money, consists of national party contributions to candidates *plus* coordinated party expenditures. Similar regressions are then estimated, separating the two types of party support: party contributions and coordinated party spending. Most of the estimated coefficients have similar signs in all three of these categories, suggesting the decision process is similiar. For that reason, estimated coefficients for race and sex variables are the only estimates reported for the disaggregated measures. These appear at the bottom of the tables.

In general, the party-unity hypothesis that political parties will allocate funds based on the candidates' voting on pro-party initiatives is not supported. In only a single case, the 1980 election for the Democratic party, the estimated coefficient on PU was significantly different from zero. As was indicated above, leaders of both parties seem to have found other means of enforcing party discipline; means that are less harmful to the parties' electorial chances. These other means of enforcing party unity, such as the use of committee assignments, have implications for an incumbent's ability to raise campaign funds. Moreover, they are less likely to decrease party numbers in the House, although supportive members can still be rewarded. Our results are not completely compatible with those of Leyden and Borrelli (1990) who found that in 1984,

Table 6.1
Determinants of Contributions by the Democratic Party, National Party,
and Coordinated Party Spending: Incumbents

	1980	1982	1984	1986	1988
PU	.0252*	-.0122	-.0157	.0458	-.0312
	(.0143)	(.0461)	(.0605)	(.0583)	(.0772)
LASTVOTE	-.3103	-6.2704	-15.1888*	-8.4560*	-33.0623
	(1.9594)	(6.1003)	(7.9603)	(4.7123)	(6.3942)
VOTEGAP	-10.1963***	-35.2849***	-11.8127	-19.9005***	-23.8717***
	(2.5731)	(8.5474)	(7.2637)	(5.8506)	(6.3404)
OPSPEND	.0163***	.0165***	.0477***	.0186***	.0242***
	(.0019)	(.0047)	(.0048)	(.0041)	(.0054)
BLACK	.5975	1.2833	-4.2125	-.5734	-2.1846
	(1.1922)	(3.2323)	(3.6859)	(2.4487)	(2.9288)
FEMALE	.2679	-6.8910*	3.6756	.4005	4.6551
	(1.2733)	(4.0941)	(3.6605)	(2.9974)	(3.5304)

National Party Spending only

	1980	1982	1984	1986	1988
BLACK	.4321	-3.3695	-2.5941	-.5556	-.2792
	(.8419)	(2.8982)	(2.2800)	(1.2619)	(1.1822)
FEMALE	.3824	-3.1194	1.4878	-.4779	.7954
	(.8987)	(2.5494)	(2.0254)	(1.5328)	(1.4462)

Coordinated Party Spending only

	1980	1982	1984	1986	1988
BLACK	-.8819	3.8076	-2.8135	.8828	-1.8660
	(4.3810)	(3.9899)	(3.5450)	(2.4670)	(3.1800)
FEMALE	-4.9234	-7.2456	3.9546	2.7609	4.7213
	(9.3379)	(12.9294)	(3.4544)	(2.3907)	(3.5959)

Standard errors appear in parentheses below the estimated coefficients.
* indicates significance at the .10 α-level, ** at the .05 α-level, and
*** at the .01 α-level.

Democratic committees appeared to use party loyalty as one criterion for contribution decisions.

The sign of the coefficient on the voting percentages in the previous election, (LASTVOTE), is negative in all five election cycles for both parties in the incumbents' equations. These coefficients are significant in over half the cases. At the same time this variable is almost always

Table 6.2
Determinants of Contributions by the Republican Party, National Party, and Coordinated Party Spending: Incumbents

	1980	1982	1984	1986	1988
PU	.0304	.0166	.0316	.0188	-.0205
	(.0129)	(.0849)	(.0766)	(.0646)	(.0640)
LASTVOTE	-5.9502	-24.9447**	-20.9348**	-31.2652***	-30.8040***
	(3.9403)	(9.4094)	(10.5784)	(10.7166)	(8.1767)
VOTEGAP	-14.5755***	-65.0340***	-56.1305***	-36.2892***	-13.9409***
	(5.8281)	(13.2433)	(12.8169)	(9.5625)	(10.0312)
OPSPEND	.0332***	.0401***	.0453***	.0535***	.0600***
	(.0057)	(.0057)	(.0074)	(.0062)	(.0052)
FEMALE	-1.8176	-2.2896	7.5931	-3.8507	-.9313
	(2.8158)	(6.0155)	(5.4945)	(4.2867)	(3.9406)

National Party Spending only

FEMALE	-.4795	3.2442*	2.7681**	1.9572	.2236
	(1.5089)	(1.8075)	(1.3908)	(1.3103)	(1.2984)

Coordinated Party Spending only

FEMALE	-.8540	-7.7325	15.3848*	-.2094	5.2441
	(5.9182)	(9.8180)	(11.3797)	(8.9979)	(8.1367)

Standard errors appear in parentheses below the estimated coefficients.
* indicates significance at the .10 α -level, ** at the .05 α -level, and
*** at the .01 α -level.

positive (two exceptions) in the nonincumbent regressions although the negative estimates are not significantly different from zero. This sign switch was predicted.

The VOTEGAP hypothesis, that close elections bring forth greater contributions from all sources including political parties, is soundly supported as all the coefficients—both parties, incumbents, and non-incumbents—in all five election cycles are negative as predicted. With a single exception these coefficients are highly significant, passing a two-tailed test at the .01 α-level. What is evident is that both Republican and Democratic strategists operate from a conservative mode of supporting candidates in close races where the money can make a difference, rather than placing their money in lopsided affairs.

Table 6.3
Determinants of Contributions by the Democratic Party, National Party, and Coordinated Party Spending: Nonincumbents

	1980	1982	1984	1986	1988
OPEN	1.8642	-0.8514	6.4385***	-2.7025	3.7919
	(1.2157)	(1.1715)	(2.2900)	(2.2881)	(3.1882)
LASTVOTE	3.5822	3.5307	3.9782	9.0468	-8.3245
	(2.9639)	(2.8571)	(5.3161)	(5.8728)	(7.7030)
VOTEGAP	-46.8117***	-48.3008***	-60.4414***	-98.6797***	-159.0017***
	(5.9437)	(6.8714)	(10.4553)	(11.2795)	(16.5038)
OPSPEND	.0005*	.0104***	.0175***	.0107***	.0074*
	(.0027)	(.0029)	(.0045)	(.0033)	(.0039)
BLACK	6.7565**	-1.6176	10.6298**	14.8512***	9.6167
	(2.8261)	(3.1119)	(5.3198)	(5.5650)	(9.8723)
FEMALE	1.8739	-1.0266	.6727	-3.7095	-2.4520
	(1.5302)	(1.7569)	(2.4165)	(2.9818)	(3.2227)

National Party Spending only

	1980	1982	1984	1986	1988
BLACK	4.3854***	-.4600	2.7746	4.5367*	5.5791*
	(1.8301)	(1.9743)	(3.0543)	(2.5970)	(4.0257)
FEMALE	.2005	-.8032	.7577	-2.3243	-.2678
	(1.0154)	(1.1305)	(1.4347)	(1.5092)	(1.3540)

Coordinated Party Spending only

	1980	1982	1984	1986	1988
BLACK	11.9199*	-.4219	8.6445**	13.0853***	7.7138
	(7.0483)	(3.3037)	(3.8758)	(4.5103)	(9.0035)
FEMALE	7.3904**	-1.1626	.2069	-2.8724	-2.5478
	(3.7001)	(1.9386)	(1.7706)	(2.4816)	(3.0267)

Standard errors appear in parentheses below the estimated coefficients.
* indicates significance at the .10 α-level, ** at the .05 α-level, and
*** at the .01 α-level.

Throughout this investigation a central theoretical result has sustained its validity even though it challenges the conventional wisdom in some ways. Viewing elections as a rent-seeking game leads to the conclusion that candidates will respond to increased spending by their opposition (OPPONENT$). This expectation is supported as the opponent's expenditures has a positive and significant impact on the candidates contributions in every regression.

Table 6.4
Determinants of Contributions by the Republican Party, National Party, and Coordinated Party Spending: Nonincumbents

	1980	1982	1984	1986	1988
OPEN	9.5920***	9.0265***	9.5935**	17.9669***	22.9848***
	(2.6104)	(3.4670)	(4.8400)	(4.0517)	(5.7660)
LASTVOTE	13.4252**	9.5025	33.7144***	-10.9151	12.9780
	(6.5518)	(8.4444)	(12.6065)	(9.2065)	(11.9032)
VOTEGAP	-118.6268***	-204.7147***	-217.4885***	-230.7929***	-182.1630***
	(11.6268)	(19.4132)	(21.2329)	(20.7929)	(21.2982)
OPSPEND	.0304***	.0267***	.0296***	.0160***	.0404***
	(.0062)	(.0075)	(.0077)	(.0054)	(.0067)
BLACK	-4.4027	8.4645	17.1339**		
	(5.6970)	(6.8748)	(7.6255)		
FEMALE	6.0423**	4.4396	-1.2884	5.6406	2.8872
	(3.0389)	(4.9930)	(4.5329)	(4.5426)	(6.4560)

National Party Spending only

	1980	1982	1984	1986	1988
BLACK	-2.3289	3.3076	4.1715		
	(2.9695)	(2.6755)	(2.9573)		
FEMALE	3.5261**	.0148	.2928	3.0659*	2.1067
	(1.7022)	(1.9970)	(1.7520)	(1.7625)	(2.4356)

Coordinated Party Spending only

	1980	1982	1984	1986	1988
BLACK	-12.3337	5.8467	17.4722**		
	(9.3651)	(7.7846)	(8.5418)		
FEMALE	1.8231	7.3121	-.9668	-.1773	-5.3739
	(3.5017)	(4.9935)	(4.7496)	(6.7356)	(11.2763)

Standard errors appear in parentheses below the estimated coefficients.
* indicates significance at the .10 α-level, ** at the .05 α-level, and
*** at the .01 α-level.

Open-seat races tend to attract more political money as attested to by the coefficients on OPEN in the nonincumbent regressions. Interestingly, the Republican party appears to be much more interested in financing open-seat races than is the Democratic party. Perhaps the marginal benefit of an additional seat is greater for a minority party.

This brings us to the race and sex results. In general, candidates' race and sex appears to make little difference to political parties in the decision to contribute money to incumbents. However, this is not the case for nonincumbents. In several election cycles the race and/or sex of the nonincumbent candidate was statistically different from zero. For example, the Democratic party gave significantly *greater* contributions to black candidates than to their white counterparts in three of the five election cycles studied. The amount of the racial benefit was between $4,000 and $12,000 in the aggregate financial regressions.[6] Concentrating exclusively on party contributions, the size of the disparity shrinks, but there are still three elections with significantly greater contributions to black nonincumbent candidates. Coordinated spending by the Democratic party for black candidates is also positive and significant in three elections. The Republican party channeled significantly greater resources to black challengers in a single election year, 1984.

Throughout the decade, black incumbents received nominal support from the Democratic party (all black incumbent representatives were Democrats). Only Mike Espey (MS 2) obtained substantial support in his re-election bid in 1988. Espy had defeated Webb Franklin in a hard fought race in 1986 and the Republican party was determined to regain the seat. The Democratic party met their challenge with $56,216 in contributions and spending, considerably above the $9,005 average. On the other hand, most black incumbents, with the possible exception of Ron Dellums (CA 8) were secure and often had only token opposition. While it may have been tempting for black congressional leaders Augustus Hawkins (CA 29) or William Gray (PA 2) to draw on party coffers, Hawkins received no party money during the eighties while Gray received $7,797 in 1986 and $3,862 in 1988. Only in 1982, when he faced a tougher than usual challenge from Claude Hutchison, did Dellums receive significant party aid; party-coordinated spending of $16,164. Dellums, however, has been regarded as a maverick, and so congressional party leaders have been less inclined to support him.

As regression results indicate, the Democratic party has put money into supporting the broadening of black representation in Congress, providing strong financial support to black challengers and open-seat candidates. The Republican party has been less forthcoming in part because many black Republican challengers ran against well-entrenched, black Democratic incumbents, creating a nearly hopeless situation. Democratic party spending (direct and indirect) of $10,757 helped Alan Wheat (MO 5) to win the open seat left vacant when Richard Bolling retired from Congress in 1982. In 1986, Democratic spending of $42,841 fueled Faye Williams's losing effort to gain the open seat left behind when Cathy Long (LA 8) retired.[7] The Democratic party had earlier targeted the majority black Mississippi Second District in 1982 with $6,400 for Robert Charles's losing challenge in 1982 and $52,000 when he challenged Franklin again in 1984. Democratic support finally paid off in 1986 when Mike Espey won the seat. Black challengers and open-seat candidates did not always fare as well at Democratic party hands. In 1982, Henry Michaux's try for the open North Carolina Second District seat received no party money, and John Lewis won the seat vacated by Wyche Fowler (GA 5), when he moved to the Senate in 1986, with only $446 in party support.

Black Republican challengers and open-seat candidates usually found themselves pitted against black Democrats in inner-city districts. Republican party officials might be questioned as to the wisdom of contributing $2,000 to William White's challenge to Bill Clay (MO 1) in 1980 when White could obtain only $700 in corporate PAC money and received only 29.8 percent of the vote. In other situations Republican support was more substantial. Republicans provided $8,609 to Claiborne Smothers as he challenged Martin Frost (TX 24), and in 1984 provided $45,940 to Lucy Patterson when she took on Frost. Other favored challengers in 1982 included John Conway (MA 10), who received $30,582 which was 16.6 percent of his receipts, and Shirley Gissendaner (CA 44) who obtained $29,505 (46.5 percent of her total) that year. Ron Dellums has often been targeted by the Republican party, and so when a black candidate came forward in 1984, the party opened its coffers to the tune of $51,909.[8] The party also provided $53,063 (44.7 percent of the total) to Joseph Watkins's losing challenge to Andrew Jacobs (IN 10) in 1984. More typical of Republican support was the zero financial support for Michael Hirt, who challenged Augustus Hawkins in 1980; Alan Shatteen, who challenged Louis Stokes (OH 21) in 1982; or Dan Cheeks, who challenged Cardiss Collins (IL 7) in 1982.[9] All three of these latter Democratic incumbents are black. While black Republican challengers and open-seat candidates run in tough races, without party support they are doomed to failure, and without party support or the likelihood of support other black Republicans are unlikely to come forward to contest the seats in subsequent elections.

Consistent with the results of PAC contributions, there are few differences in contributions based on gender. One election, 1982, found the Democratic party contributing less money to female candidates, but no other significant difference arises in the other years. The Republican party results suggest a gender difference for incumbents, with a $2,700 (1984) to $3,200 (1982) increase to female incumbent candidates.

Nonincumbent results are similar. The Democratic party increased coordinated expenditures in support of female candidates in the 1980 elections, but no other elections had significant results. Nonincumbent Republican female candidates received greater party contributions in 1980 and 1986. Otherwise, the Republican party did not appear to take gender into account when making a contributions decision.

More women than blacks ran for Congress in the 1980s, and it appears both parties were more supportive of female than black candidates. For example, in 1980 Bobbi Fiedler's (CA 21) challenger victory was funded in part (9.7 percent of her total receipts) by Republican support of $57,776. Two other Republican challengers that year, Marge Roukema (NJ 7) and Claudine Schneider (RI 2) also found support at Republican hands that year, receiving $49,578 and $42,609 respectively, while Naomi Bradford's open-seat (CO 1) effort received $66,269. In 1982, the Republican party poured $52,998 into Sissy Baker's losing attempt at gaining the open Tennessee fourth district in a battle with Jim Cooper, another Tennessean of notable political lineage. The party money was only 4.4 percent of Baker's receipts in the high-spending race, but the Republican support of $53,722 was 25.55 percent of Helen Delich Bentley's receipts as she lost her challenge to gain the Maryland Second District seat.[10] Notable in 1984 was Republican party support of $27,938 to Suzanne Warner in her losing challenge to Romano Mazzoli (KY 3) because it was 94.4 percent of her total receipts.

With much less money the Democrats, nonetheless, put $30,195 into Jane Wells-Schooley's (PA 15) losing effort in 1984. In 1986, Republican efforts went over the $100,000 mark as the party provided $115,307 (21.6 percent of her receipts) to Patricia Saiki's (HI 1) successful open-seat campaign. That same year Kathleen Kennedy Townsend raised $1,076,271 to challenge Helen Bentley, but the Democratic party provided only $4,100 support for her losing race while the Republicans provided $51,477 of Bentley's $1,071,649 war chest. Party support to women was down in absolute dollar amounts in 1986. This same trend continued in 1988. Although Republican and Democratic incumbent and nonincumbent women often received sizable party support, they usually raised larger sums from other sources. Party contributions, even when large, as was the $36,531 the Democratic party provided to help Liz Patterson (SC 4) retain her seat against a tough challenger in 1988, were only a small part of her $974,466 war chest. As was the case with black incumbents, female incumbents tended to receive less party support unless they were in tough re-election battles, reflecting their ability to raise funds elsewhere.

In conclusion, two central results stand out. First, political parties appear to place incumbent candidates on an equal footing in terms of financial support regardless of race and gender. Second, while race and gender seem to matter to parties to a greater extent for nonincumbent candidates, the differentials are usually positive. In other words, both political parties appear to be inclined to channel *greater* amounts of resources to black and female candidates than to their white/male counterparts.

While campaign contributions are not subject to equal opportunity and affirmative-action regulations, political parties appear to have adopted philosophies yielding results similar to those policies. For women and blacks this is probably welcome news, but a serious obstacle remains: the inertia of incumbency. Black and female challengers may actually receive greater contributions than do white/male challengers, but this improves their chances of winning only marginally. It is incumbents who have a lock on winning, and the vast majority of Congress remains white and male.

It is also somewhat incongruous to suggest the Republican party does not consider race when there were *no* black Republican incumbents in the decade, and there were no black Republican candidates of any status in 1988. Clearly, race matters in American politics, but its direct impact on party finances is small.

NOTES

1. The literature on the role of the parties is vast. Two works that clearly enunciate the decline of the parties thesis, with further references, are William Crotty and Gary Jacobson (1980) and Wattenberg (1986).

2. Notice that these benefit seekers are not analogous to the rent-seekers we introduced in chapter 4. They are indeed rent-seekers, but so are the winners that Schlesinger introduces.

3. Party leaders, of course, recognize the need for representatives to vote the district on some issues even if the vote conflicts with party goals.

4. An exception would be a permanent, ideologically driven minority. This party is an exception to the Downsian thesis because its goal is not actually to control the legislature (although it would be happy to do so). Instead, this party sees its goal as the pursuit of a particular ideology. It will content itself with small victories and the ability to spread its particular ideology.

5. This strategy is often weakened because the people controlling congressional campaign funds are up for re-election and may channel monies into their own campaigns.

6. Once again, some candidates received no financial aid and a tobit routine is employed. Comparing these tobit estimates with OLS results revealed small differ-

ences in both significance levels and magnitude. Hence, our discussion proceeds as if these coefficients are partials.

7. Williams received $26,338 in Democratic support when she ran again as a challenger in 1988.

8. The Republican party provided a contribution of only $1,107 to Dellums's black challenger in 1980.

9. The Republican party did provide $24,665 to James Bevel when he challenged Collins in 1984.

10. Bentley won in 1984 with $70,091 in party support.

Chapter Seven

Individual Contributors and Discrimination

While the composition of campaign contributions has changed radically in the last twenty years, a constant has been the dominance of individual contributions. Campaign contributions from individuals still make up the lion's share of aggregate contributions. This does not mean, however, that contributions from individuals dominate every candidate's financial situation. Indeed, as Table 7.1 shows, the importance of individual contributions is dependent on candidate status.

Since 1980, the level of individual contributions has continued to rise for both incumbents and nonincumbents, but the proportion of total contributions made up of individual contributions has varied. After 1984, individual contributions make up a declining portion of incumbents' campaign finances, but are of increasing importance for nonincumbents.[1] A decline in the proportion of individual contributions during a period of growth in their absolute levels suggests institutional funds are growing more rapidly. Comparing Table 7.1 with aggregate figures on PAC contributions in Table 5.1 demonstrates how far this shift has gone. After 1984, individual contributions were no longer the primary source of money for incumbents; they were replaced by contributions from PACs, and the differential continues to grow.

Individual contributions do not lend themselves to modeling as readily as do other types of contributions. Contributions by political groups, be it political parties or interest groups, can be approached theoretically by assuming they behave as if a single decision maker is optimizing an identifiable objective function. That approach is not tenable for individual

Table 7.1
Average Individual Contributions and Their Proportion of Total Contributions

| | Individual Contributions | | Percent of Total Contributions | |
	Incumbents	Nonincumbents	Incumbents	Nonincumbents
1980*	$108,100	$80,600	54.4%	70.0%
1982*	$163,100	$112,900	54.3%	63.6%
1984	$149,125	$81,000	43.8%	40.5%
1986	$173,800	$103,000	42.8%	44.0%
1988	$184,000	$109,300	40.7%	45.4%

*Individual contributions were calculated differently in 1980 and 1982 by the FEC. The primary difference is the inclusion of a candidate's own contributions to his or her own campaign.

contributors because the possible goals of contributors are as profuse as their numbers.

In addition, a theory explaining the motivation of an individual who contributes money to a congressional campaign faces the public-choice voting dilemma. It is difficult to state a rational explanation as to why people vote in elections. The probability that an individual's vote will influence an election is vanishingly small, and yet there are costs to voting. Theoretically, as Anthony Downs (1957) shows, no rational person should be expected to vote. Many individual contributors, especially small contributors responding to direct mail, pose the same dilemma. A contribution of $10 is a miniscule proportion of a representative's campaign portfolio giving the contributor no discernable political return, yet it imposes a cost.

This public-choice dilemma has not been satisfactorily resolved, and it may ultimately prove to be inscrutable. Geoffrey Brennan and James Buchanan cast doubt on the entire theoretical foundation of public-choice analysis when they challenge the orthodoxy that voters act rationally. They claim that the assumption that voters "act purposively to secure their particular individual ends (1984, 185)" is unsubstantiated. Instead, they posit a more vague motive for voters that essentially assumes voters vote because the act of voting yields utility. Elegantly stated by Brennan and Buchanan,

People vote because they want to—period. And they vote how they want—period. And neither the act of voting nor the direction of a vote cast can be explained as a means to achieving a particular political outcome, any more than spectators attend a game as a means of securing the victory of their team. (1984, 187)

Small individual campaign contributions can be viewed in the same fashion. An individual sends $25 to a particular candidate because she wants to do so. That this contribution will have no effect on the election is irrelevant to the contributor as she has derived some sort of utility from her gift.

Larger individual campaign contributions, on the order of $1,000–$2,000, are a different matter.[2] Often, contributions of this size entail personal contact with the candidate, which has a potential of developing into an exchange relationship where the views of the contributor may be given consideration by the elected official. Unfortunately, even if a "rational" motive can be ascribed to these contributors, the diverse nature of their potential views eliminates the possibility of identifying an objective function to model their behavior.

In lieu of an identifiable goal or objective, a model of individual contributions requires a different approach. The tack taken here relies on the usefulness of information. An actual objective function used by individuals to make contribution decisions may not be discernable, but it can be assumed that regardless of an individual's goals, information is useful. This suggests informational measures should be related to individual contributions. Second, the ability to contribute is a constraint placed on contributors affecting the level of contributions regardless of their particular objectives. This framework can be used to generate empirical hypotheses that can then be tested.

A MODEL OF INDIVIDUAL CAMPAIGN CONTRIBUTIONS

First, assume elements of the population receive utility from the act of contributing money to congressional campaigns and that this utility is related to a candidate receiving the contribution.[3] Second, assume preferences for candidates with particular attributes are disbursed randomly throughout the population. Under these circumstances certain individuals will contribute to particular candidates. Our interest in these contributions then branches in two directions: What factors increase or decrease the size of contributions or the number of contributions? What factors determine to whom the contributions go?[4]

Factors affecting both the level and dispersion of individual contributions fit into two categories: informational characteristics and demographic traits of the district. Information about candidates can be quite basic, that a candidate is running and wants money; or more specific, such as party affiliation, previous election results, race, and sex. Demographics become important because preferences may be randomly distributed but the population is not. Particular congressional districts have wealthier populations, less-well-educated people, or exhibit other population traits likely to affect contributions.[5] Using these categories, the determinants of the expected level of contributions for a candidate can be efficiently expressed as:

$$INDIV\$ = f \text{ (utility, information, demographics)}. \qquad (7.1)$$

The utility component is unmeasurable, but assuming this utility does not differ systematically with candidates (for reasons other than the explicitly included variables), the remaining characteristics of interest in this study can be evaluated.

Information comes in many colors, and several variables are included to capture assorted shades. One hue reflects candidates' need for funds. Candidates with a greater desire for additional money are expected to search for contributors more diligently, increasing both the number of requests made and changing the manner of solicitation. All else equal, when a candidate increases the number and type of pleas for funds, the cost of a contribution to a contributor declines. In other words, by providing more opportunities to contribute, it becomes easier to contribute. The cost of contributions is defined as the ease with which contributions can be made. For example, suppose an individual is on the margin of contributing to a campaign. If he receives a mail request containing a self-addressed stamped return envelope, he is more likely to write a check than if he needs to find, address, and stamp an envelope, a situation known to all direct-mail practitioners. The size of particular contributions are affected similarly. For example, suppose a potential contributor is able and willing to give a large contribution. If she has the opportunity to meet and talk with the candidate, the resulting contribution often grows. Therefore, candidates with a greater desire for funds are likely to make themselves more available to contributors, and contributions are expected to grow.

Two types of variables have been used consistently in this work to reflect candidate funding desires: those possessing information on expenditures and those indicating the closeness of the race. As one candidate spends more money on an election, an opponent has little option but to offset these expenditures with increased expenditures of his own. This situation leads to an expectation of a positive sign for the coefficient of OPPONENT$. Also included in the model is RATIO$, a measure of the candidate's spending relative to the total spending of both candidates in the election. This ratio is a reflection of the probability of winning for equally matched candidates as defined in the theory presented in chapter 4. As this probability increases or when one candidate is better financed than another, there are two opposing forces bearing on further fund-raising. Superior finances leads to greater name recognition, giving potential contributors a source for further contributions. At the same time, a leading candidate may feel less desire to push for additional funds. On the other hand, few candidates seem to think they have enough campaign money if the race is at all close. Because these possibilities may offset one another, no prediction is made for the coefficient on RATIO$.

Three tight-race measures are included, VOTEGAP, measuring the size of the vote margin in this election; OPEN, for open-seat races; and LASTVOTE, consisting of the previous election's results (all variables are defined more explicitly in the appendix at the end of the book). As before, the expected impact of LASTVOTE depends on candidate status. Close previous races are often considered to be evidence of incumbents' vulnerability. In response, candidates may seek additional donors and recontact previous contributors. Challengers are encouraged if the incumbent had a close shave in the previous election, and they redouble their efforts as well. For these reasons the expected coefficient on LASTVOTE is negative for incumbents and positive for challengers. VOTEGAP is expected to have a negative coefficient because the larger the vote discrepancy, the more secure an incumbent. OPEN is expected to be positive as open-seat races produce maximum effort by both candidates as each scents victory.

The second group of candidate characteristics includes party affiliation, race, and sex. The impact of party affiliation on contributions from individuals is not clear. On the one hand, if the old adage that the Republican party is the party of the rich rings true, the sign on DEMO-CRAT would be negative. On the other hand, the Democratic party often has more registered voters and numbers may increase contributions. For these conflicting reasons, no sign is predicted for the coefficient on DEMOCRAT a priori. Race and sex characteristics are central to this study, but because we cannot measure the utility generated by a contribution to (or in opposition to) a black or female candidate, no predictions can be made for these variables. We can, however, observe the resulting contributions to see if funding differentials are statistically discernable. These estimated coefficients will suggest whether or not individual contributors are concerned about candidates' gender and skin color.

Demographic characteristics of the candidates' districts are included because some districts may have a population more likely to contribute to congressional campaigns than are the populations of other districts. Realizing the potential importance of demographic characteristics, a decision as to which characteristics should be included arises. Aid is available for this selection because there is a rich literature on the determinants of political participation. Those studies (cited later) guide our selection of variables.

Most of the political participation literature specifically investigates voting. Certainly the decision to contribute is different from the decision to vote, but both can be viewed as points on a continuum of participation. With that perspective, it may well be that the characteristics enhancing voting participation are related to participation of another sort: contributing to campaigns. Verba and Nie (1972), Wolfinger and Rosenstone (1980), Paul Abramson (1983), Shienbaum (1984), and Margaret Conway (1991) cite several determinants of voting participation including education, income, and age.[6] These indicators become our central district demographic measures of the likelihood of monetary participation.

Three district measures are included in our study through the medium of district aggregates. Specifically, the median age of the population of the district creates the variable, AGEPOP, median income is INCOMPOP, and median education, EDUCPOP. It is important to note that voter participation studies differ significantly from this work because they use voter-specific information derived from survey data while this study uses districtwide aggregates. Therefore, the estimates calculated here cannot be used to make inferences about individual behavior. However, excluding these district differences could attribute contribution decisions to inappropriate variables.

The coefficient on AGEPOP is expected to be positive due to the findings of a positive relationship between voter participation and age (Verba and Nie 1972, Shienbaum 1984). The usual perception is that the likelihood of voting increases from a low in the early twenties and remains high until people are nearly seventy. INCOMPOP is also expected to have a positive coefficient in both the incumbents' and nonincumbents' equations as the opportunity cost of contributions is lower for wealthier people. In addition, higher-income people are generally perceived (e.g., Wolfinger and Rosenstone 1980, Abramson 1983) to be more likely to vote and particpate in other ways than are lower-income people. Finally, EDUCPOP is also expected to have a positive coefficient based on the positive influence that education generally has on participation (Conway 1991).

Because education and income are highly correlated, the inclusion of both EDUCPOP and INCOMPOP in the same equation creates a serious multicollinearity problem. This can inflate the standard errors and disrupt significance tests (Studenmund and Cassidy 1987). Therefore, each regression equation is estimated twice; once with IN-COMPOP and again substituting EDUCPOP. As the estimated coefficients and significance levels of the common variables differ only in minor ways, a single set of results are reported. Tables 7.2–7.5 present the estimates using the INCOMPOP specification. Included in these tables are coefficient estimates of EDUCPOP. They are presented in brackets to remind the reader that INCOMPOP and EDUCPOP come from separate regressions.

Another district attribute included as an explanatory variable is the percentage of the population made up of blacks, BLACKPOP. Estimates of this characteristic on individual contributions is of interest for two distinct reasons. First, Verba and Nie (1972) suggested blacks have lower voter participation rates than do whites on the average, and so the racial composition of a district may also affect individual contributions. Shingles (1981) has questioned this conclusion, but Abramson and Clagett (1984) continue to argue that black Americans participate less than do whites of the same socioeconomic status. Second, black candidates primarily run in districts with a large, often majority-black population. The possibility of an affinity between black candidates and black contributors is measured by this variable.

The investigation of individuals' contributions to congressional campaigns takes the form of the following regressions:

INDIV\$ = f (OPPONENT\$, RATIO\$, VOTEGAP, LASTVOTE, OPEN,

   (+)   (?)   (–)   (–, +)   (+)

DEMOCRAT, INCOMPOP, [EDUCPOP], AGEPOP, BLACK,

   (?)   (+)   [+]   (+)   (?)

FEMALE, BLACKPOP).

   (?)   (?)   (7.2)

Depending upon candidate status, the information carried by some of the explanatory variables differs. In other words, incumbents may face one set of expectations, and contributors are expected to treat them differently than they treat nonincumbents. For this reason, equation (7.2)

Table 7.2
Determinants of Individual Contributions: Incumbents

	1980	1982	1984	1986	1988
RATIOSP	413.811***	416.742***	361.342***	492.409***	481.008***
	(41.381)	(55.374)	(47.865)	(83.329)	(69.834)
OPPONENT$	.8284***	.4748***	.4651***	.7011***	.5903***
	(.0542)	(.0415)	(.0422)	(.0674)	(.0600)
VOTEGAP	-213.929***	-310.439***	-143.197***	-149.283*	-175.420***
	(57.147)	(75.631)	(49.813)	(49.774)	(64.437)
LASTVOTE	-56.274	-66.705	-140.818***	-89.161	-90.487*
	(37.620)	(49.179)	(45.069)	(64.423)	(55.278)
DEMOCRAT	-26.812**	39.002***	-26.960***	-23.748	-25.862*
	(11.064)	(14.604)	(10.339)	(16.713)	(15.221)
INCOMPOP	-2.664	2.311	3.878***	5.149***	6.383***
	(2.639)	(1.664)	(1.269)	(2.142)	(2.009)
[EDUCPOP]	-.1933	64.480***	91.510***	119.374***	115.354***
	(.4507)	(22.043)	(19.899)	(26.215)	(25.461)
AGEPOP	-1.580	-1.230	2.526	5.085**	4.767**
	(1.762)	(2.548)	(1.761)	(2.504)	(2.225)
BLACK	-24.180	-42.314	8.791***	-42.762	44.728
	(34.459)	(42.435)	(23.080)	(35.509)	(44.731)
FEMALE	27.276	-42.314	19.387	-42.762*	-2.807
	(26.247)	(42.435)	(23.080)	(26.629)	(30.451)
BLACKPOP	.4900	.3302**	1.8875***	1.166*	-.7747
	(.4800)	(.1533)	(.4187)	(.6594)	(.7235)

Individual contributions in 1980 and 1984 include contributions to one's own campaign.
The standard error of the estimate lies below the estimated coefficient in parentheses.
* indicates significance at the .10 α-level, ** at the .05 α-level,
and *** at the .01 α-level.

is estimated two times for each election cycle with data for incumbents in one case and nonincumbent data in the other. The results are reported in separate tables.

Estimating coefficients for the explanatory variables given in equation (7.2) should help us identify dominant factors affecting the level of individual contributions. This is, however, an incomplete picture of a candidate's dependence on this particular source of funds. Individual

Table 7.3
Determinants of Individual Contributions: Nonincumbents
Tobit Estimates

	1980	1982	1984	1986	1988
RATIOSP	324.763***	592.394***	408.819***	509.042***	502.492***
	(8.698)	(11.327)	(23.659)	(31.227)	(35.769)
	172.904	310.532	226.119	277.901	271.269
OPPONENT$	.3433***	.4462***	.3073***	.2220***	.1807***
	(.0216)	(.0364)	(.0208)	(.0191)	(.0194)
	.1828	.2339	.1687	.1208	.1013
VOTEGAP	-44.706	21.856**	39.356	43.828	-142.440**
	(46.145)	(8.644)	(57.239)	(69.497)	(75.119)
	-23.706	11.457	12.339	19.424	-93.396
LASTVOTE	-31.881	122.112***	2.484	91.594***	50.692*
	(23.149)	(37.869)	(30.323)	(32.419)	(30.169)
	-16.973	64.011	3.207	49.743	28.975
DEMOCRAT	7.673	25.420*	-19.445***	.302	-30.239***
	(7.065)	(13.133)	(7.448)	(10.294)	(10.402)
	4.085	13.325	-9.696	.198	-17.518
OPEN	-14.932	-6.582	-.901	-4.121	-12.935
	(9.463)	(15.981)	(11.883)	(14.408)	(17.641)
	-7.950	-3.450	-.853	-1.989	-9.206
INCOMPOP	3.095*	2.308	1.148	2.321*	2.434*
	(1.647)	(1.659)	(.947)	(1.363)	(1.400)
	1.648	1.210	.773	1.317	.122
[EDUCPOP]	.239	28.847	30.643*	42.032**	41.232**
	(.338)	(21.188)	(16.899)	(17.970)	(18.239)
	.127	15.122	17.056	23.105	22.884
AGEPOP	.034	3.235	1.539	1.726	1.700
	(.054)	(.709)	(1.399)	(2.038)	(1.700)
	.018	1.696	.996	.949	.944
BLACK	-1.292	-48.995	-24.497	-119.042**	-61.897
	(21.945)	(35.153)	(22.359)	(48.152)	(70.837)
	-.687	-25.683	-16.583	-66.137	-28.994
FEMALE	-5.621	-17.579	-11.515	17.251	15.775
	(11.197)	(22.285)	(11.500)	(16.031)	(16.945)
	-2.993	-9.215	-7.210	10.119	8.806
BLACKPOP	-.5741	.4458	.2882	.2624	-.1259
	(.3278)	(.5611)	(.3371)	(.4176)	(.4553)
	-.3030	.2337	.1604	.1650	-.0650

The standard error lies below the estimated coefficient in parentheses, and the bottom
number in each triad is the estimated partial derivative; see equation [5.5].
* indicates significance at the .10 α-level, ** at the .05 α-level,
and *** at the .01 α-level.

Table 7.4
Determinants of Large Individual Contributions*: Incumbents

	1980	1982	1984	1986	1988
RATIOSP	114.163***	147.942***	199.907***	326.161***	208.170***
	(14.708)	(22.043)	(27.252)	(51.652)	(38.565)
OPPONENT$	.2506***	.1514***	.2346***	.3186***	.2508***
	(.0192)	(.0165)	(.0240)	(.0417)	(.0331)
VOTEGAP	-26.862	-104.562***	-48.722*	-170.455***	-30.424
	(20.473)	(30.107)	(28.360)	(49.448)	(35.585)
LASTVOTE	-23.607*	-2.173	-31.461	6.898	-11.631
	(13.417)	(19.577)	(25.659)	(39.933)	(31.519)
DEMOCRAT	2.302	13.063**	-4.107	-8.874	.053
	(3.945)	(5.814)	(5.886)	(10.360)	(8.405)
INCOMPOP	-1.323	1.358**	1.430**	3.533***	4.865****
	(.939)	(.662)	(.723)	(1.328)	(1.109)
[EDUCPOP]	-.043	17.158***	22.377***	41.992***	44.812***
	(.105)	(5.434)	(6.453)	(9.711)	(8.490)
AGEPOP	-.0955	.1931	.4860	.3748**	2.2304**
	(.0627)	(1.0145)	(1.002)	(1.5544)	(1.2530)
BLACK	-22.396*	-37.844**	-13.379	-46.868	-18.240
	(12.294)	(16.893)	(13.468)	(30.943)	(24.702)
FEMALE	2.448	-14.113	-2.300	-26.193	3.710
	(9.329)	(11.875)	(13.005)	(22.011)	(16.816)
BLACKPOP	.2460	.5035**	1.049***	.974**	.313
	(.177)	(.244)	(.238)	(.485)	(.399)

Large individual contributions are defined as those greater than $500.00.
The standard error of the estimate lies below the estimated coefficient in parentheses.
* indicates significance at the .10 α-level, ** at the .05 α-level,
and *** at the .01 α-level.

contributions come in vastly different sizes, ranging from a few dollars
to thousands of dollars, and there are reasons to expect that large and
small contributors differ in their determination of candidate suitability
for funding. Even though the FECA prohibited huge individual contributions to candidates of the size of $1 million or more that were made
in the past, individual contributors have been increasing the size of their

Table 7.5
Determinants of Large Individual Contributions*: Nonincumbents
Tobit Estimates

	1980	1982	1984	1986	1988
RATIOSP	110.166***	179.418***	231.304***	288.040***	502.491***
	(8.699)	(11.327)	(17.922)	(22.483)	(35.769)
	28.764	58.185	78.691	100.909	183.459
OPPONENT$	.144**	.091***	.184***	.125***	.181***
	(.009)	(.011)	(.016)	(.013)	(.019)
	.038	.029	.063	.044	.065
VOTEGAP	-25.349	2.089	74.108*	66.274	-142.440**
	(21.077)	(28.089)	(43.494)	(49.738)	(75.119)
	-6.186	.677	24.292	23.353	-48.683
LASTVOTE	3.593	-5.233	-7.791	45.899**	50.692
	(10.866)	(12.174)	(22.873)	(23.197)	(37.007)
	.938	-1.697	-2.264	16.173	17.814
DEMOCRAT	3.667	-12.353***	-5.590	-7.388	-30.239***
	(3.276)	(4.309)	(5.815)	(7.454)	(10.401)
	.957	-4.006	-1.815	-2.545	-10.663
OPEN	-7.429*	7.343	.364	.684	-12.936
	(4.168)	(5.123)	(8.606)	(10.182)	(17.641)
	-1.940	2.381	.169	.274	-4.251
INCOMPOP	.921	1.176**	.505	1.070	2.434*
	(.762)	(.556)	(.718)	(.996)	(1.400)
	.240	.381	.181	.304	.855
[EDUCPOP]	.073	25.105***	28.122**	31.076**	42.349***
	(.162)	(7.029)	(13.007)	(13.020)	(12.606)
	.019	8.142	9.587	10.954	15.966
AGEPOP	-.0808	.9228	2.282**	.0430	3.1960**
	(.0536)	(.7095)	(1.026)	(1.4635)	(1.4633)
	-.0210	.2993	.7908	.0152	1.205
BLACK	-9.652	-30.502**	-3.705	-87.260***	-61.897
	(11.227)	(12.486)	(16.631)	(33.958)	(70.837)
	-2.520	-9.892	-1.942	-30.506	-21.919
FEMALE	-4.143	4.0082	-13.941*	1.199	15.775
	(5.301)	(7.298)	(8.666)	(11.774)	(16.945)
	-1.082	1.2998	-4.925	.0398	5.636
BLACKPOP	.0200	.2151	.0732	-.2960	1.259
	(.0135)	(.1876)	(.2716)	(.3091)	(4.553)
	.0052	.0698	.0249	-.1160	.4173

The standard error lies below the estimated coefficient in parentheses, and the bottom number in each triad is the estimated partial derivative; see equation [5.5].
* indicates significance at the .10 α-level, ** at the .05 α-level, and *** at the .01 α-level.

contributions during the 1980s (Conlon 1987, Sorauf 1988). This situation seems to be derived from both candidate and contributor attitudes and actions. On the one hand the direct cost of obtaining many small contributions is much larger than raising the same amount of money from a few large sources. On the other hand, political IOUs exacted for large contributions may be more confining than those exchanged for small contributions, or at least contributors may think that they are getting more for their money so they are willing to increase the amount of their check. Furthermore, large contributions, of say more than $500, often involve a meeting with the candidate and may secure some access rights for the contributor in the future. Hence, large contributions may not be subject to the same "irrational" criticism public-choice theorists find in the decision to vote.

Because of these differences, "large" individual contributions, defined as contributions greater than or equal to $500, are investigated separately. Specifically, the explanatory variables in equation (7.2) are regressed on these large contributions.

Expected signs of the coefficients are identical to equation (7.2). Differences between the factors affecting all individual contributions and large, individual contributions can be explored by comparing the results of the two equations.

WHO GETS INDIVIDUAL CAMPAIGN CONTRIBUTIONS?

Estimated coefficients for the variables determining total individual contributions appear in tables 7.2 and 7.3, with the incumbent determinants in the former and nonincumbent results in the latter. Virtually every incumbent received some individual contributions, and so nonzero observations of individual contributions exist for each observation. Nonincumbents, however, included several candidates in each election with no money reported to the FEC (either because they received no contributions or because they received less than the $5,000 threshold set by the FEC for filing campaign finance reports). As before, this censored data makes OLS regression unreliable and so a tobit routine is employed.

In addition to the unmeasurable utility acquired by the individual when contributing to a campaign, individual contributions are expected to depend on information and district demographics. In general, these hypotheses are supported, although the results are stronger and more consistent for the information measures than for the district demographics.

The opponents' level of spending, OPPONENT$, is positive and strongly significant (.01 α-level) in all five elections for both incumbents and nonincumbents. This variable was also strongly significant in every election in the large-contributions category as shown in tables 7.4 and 7.5. As has been the case throughout this study, the level of opposition spending remains a key determinant of a candidate's strategy.

Another spending measure was RATIO$, which reflects the probability of a candidate winning the election, *ceteris paribus*. No a priori prediction was given for the coefficient on RATIO$ because a closer race, with RATIO$ approaching .50, would increase both candidates' desire for funds, spur additional fund-raising efforts, and increase contributions.

While our prediction for the RATIO$ variable was ambiguous, the results were not. In all five elections in both the total contributions model and the large contributions model for both incumbents and non-incumbents (a total of twenty estimates), the coefficient on RATIO$ was positive and several times its standard error.

Two close-race measures included the percentage of the vote in the last election, LASTVOTE, and the size of the win in the present election, VOTEGAP. In both sets of incumbent regressions the coefficient on VOTEGAP was negative as predicted, and it was not significant only in the 1980 and 1988 large-contributions model. For nonincumbents, however, the variable carried less distinction. Its sign fluctuated from positive to negative, and it was only intermittently significant. LASTVOTE was predicted to be dependent on the candidate's status, that is, negative for incumbents and positive for nonincumbents. In general this expectation is realized as LASTVOTE is negative in the incumbents' equations, reported in tables 7.2 and 7.4, but it is significant for only half the elections. Interestingly, LASTVOTE was significant with a large coefficient for both incumbent models in 1984. Did incumbents think themselves safe, or did potential incumbent contributions get channeled into the presidential election? Perhaps both. In the nonincumbents' equations it switches signs to become positive seven of ten times, and tended to be significant more for the general than for the large-contribution model. Large contributors to nonincumbent campaigns seem to have used gauges other than the incumbent's margin of victory in the last race.

Three district demographic measures are included to account for differences in the populations upon which candidates rely for most of their contributions.[7] Median income of the district is included to reflect the ability of people in the district to contribute to political candidates. As expected, this variable was usually positive, eighteen out of twenty times, and two-thirds of those positive coefficients are significant at the

.10 α-level. As the median income of the district rose, so did the level of individual contributions to incumbent and nonincumbent candidates. Median years of schooling attained by the population in each district is also included as participation studies (e.g., Conway 1991) suggest a positive correlation between voter participation and education. EDUCPOP was almost always positive and significant as predicted.

Because increased age is often related to participation, the median age of the population was included to see if that impact translated to contributions. This variable was a factor weaker than income or education, but in general the positive impact of age existed in the eighties. More than 75 percent of the age coefficients were positive as predicted, but slightly less than half of those were significant.

Party affiliation of the candidates is included, and while no prediction was made for this variable, it seems that Democrats receive less money than do Republicans from individuals. The Democratic disadvantage for incumbents ranged from a low of $24,000 in 1986 to a high of $33,000 in 1984 (Table 7.2). The Democratic nonincumbent disadvantage ranged from $9,600 to $17,500. Democratic incumbents and nonincumbents did receive a premium in 1982 ($39,000 for incumbents from individual contributors as a whole), probably reflecting the typical midterm decline in support for the president's party. Even though Democrats did well in the 1988 midterm elections, they did so apparently with less individual financial support. Although the DEMOCRAT variable was generally not significant in 1988, it was significant for the overall incumbent model as Democratic incumbents obtained nearly $25,000 less. Democratic incumbents had no trouble making up this shortfall in individual contributions as they turned to PACs and their party for support. Open-seat races are included in the nonincumbent equations, and while these races attracted significant increases in institutional funding (PACs and parties), they did not affect the same high level of contributions from individuals. Because open-seat candidates had a better chance of victory than did challengers, they had a better shot at institutional money and seemed to turn to these sources.

ARE INDIVIDUAL CONTRIBUTORS DISCRIMINATORY?

The results of candidates' race and sex can now be addressed. In the total individual contributions equations (Tables 7.2 and 7.3), the effects of race and sex factors were weak. The coefficient on BLACK is negative in nine of the ten cases, but it is significant only twice. These results imply black incumbents faced a $69,000 shortfall in individual contributions in the 1984 election, and black nonincumbents had a similar disadvantage of $66,000 in 1986. Both of these estimates are strongly significant, passing a .05 α-level test. However, black nonincumbents fared well with institutional sources in the 1986 election, making up for part of the shortfall.

Estimated coefficients on women candidates switch intermittently from positive to negative, and only a single estimate, for female incumbents in the 1986 election, is significantly different from zero. Table 7.2 suggests these women received $48,000 less than did their male counterparts from individual contributors after accounting for electability and district demographics. There were notable exceptions, of course. Facing a stiff challenge from Kathleen Kennedy Townsend in 1986, Helen Bentley (MD 2) raised $600,734 of her $1,071,649 from individual contributors. In a million-dollar race, candidates are forced to turn to all funding sources. Interestingly, Bentley received 41.8 percent of her contributions from individuals in the form of $500 or more per contribution.

Investigating those large, individual contributions in the aggregate supports and extends these results. First, the negative impact of race increases. In tables 7.4 and 7.5 the estimated coefficient on BLACK is negative in all five election cycles for both the incumbent sample and the nonincumbent sample. Furthermore, half of these negative coefficients are statistically significant. Incumbent black representatives received significantly lower large contributions from individuals in three of the five elections studied, with the size of the shortfall lying between $22,000 in the 1980 election and $56,000 in the 1984 election. Some black incumbents partially made up for the shortfall through other means. In 1980, William Clay (MO 1) received $45,741, or 58 percent less than the average, in the form of individual contributions, and only $3,000 of this figure came in the form of large contributions, but he received only 7 percent ($60,300) less than the average in PAC funds. Nonetheless, Clay was underfunded overall, relative to white incumbents in 1980. Nonincumbents also faced a disadvantage when attempting to raise large contributions from individuals in two elections. Adjusting for the tobit estimate to derive a partial derivative, the direct penalty of being a black nonincumbent was almost $10,000 in the 1982 election and over $30,000 in the 1986 election.

Centering on large contributions reveals additional hardship for nonincumbent women as the coefficient is now significantly negative in two election cycles. In 1984, nonincumbent women received $8,000 less than did their white male counterparts, and in 1986 the differential was a negative $5,000.

When the race or sex of a House candidate had an impact on contributions from individuals in the eighties, that impact was negative. Furthermore, this negative result was more prevalent for large contributions. These results suggest two things: first, individuals appear to discriminate against black candidates (and to a smaller extent women challengers), and second, black and female candidates appear to be dependent on smaller contributions. This latter result suggests blacks and women face greater direct fund-raising costs because raising money in small amounts from many people is more time consuming than deriving an equal amount from a few donors.

The final variable included in our regression is another district demographic measure included to see if the race of the population affects contributions. The estimated coefficients suggest incumbents running in districts with large black populations received more individual contributions than did others. In both the total individual contributions study and the large contributions regressions, the coefficient on the percentage of the population being black was positive in nine of the ten incumbent estimations. Six (1982, 1984, 1986) of those nine coefficients are significantly positive. Nonincumbents, however, appeared to face a different situation as none of the estimated coefficients were significantly different from zero.

This individual support coupled with the lower total contributions levels suggests a grim situation for candidates in black districts. These candidates apparently rely more heavily on contributions from individuals which are generally more time consuming to raise than those from institutional contributors. In addition, because the absolute level of individual contributions to black candidates is lower than those to white candidates, a black candidate who is campaigning in a black majority district (which is the case for most black candidates) faces a situation in which he has to spend more time on personal fund-raising activities and yet can expect less money for his efforts.

However, not all black incumbents are financially shortchanged. As we indicated in chapters 5 and 6, some black incumbents did very well from institutional sources. While it is true that Augustus Hawkins (CA 29) raised only $3,900 from individual contributors in 1988, he received $107,000 ($61,050 from labor PACs) of his $109,450 from PACs for that election. Hawkins ran a relatively cheap campaign by usual standards, although he still won 83 percent of the vote. As a veteran campaigner he seemed to observe the dictum, "go hunting where the ducks are," as he accepted the readily available PAC contributions without bothering to launch an intensive fund-raising effort in the district. Even more interesting is Cardiss Collins's (IL 7), the only black woman in Congress, fund-raising strategy in 1988. She obtained $22,655 (9.6 percent of the total) from individual contributors. Rather astoundingly, 86.1 percent of this figure came in contributions of more than $500, which when coupled to her PAC total of $197,778 indicates that Collins's campaign probably spent little time raising money.

As we indicated in chapter 5, Ron Dellums (CA 8) did not enjoy PAC favors during the 1980s. Hence he had to turn to individual contributors to fill his substantial war chests. His situation regarding institutional funding improved during the decade as the share of his total warchest made up by individual funds declined from 90.8 percent in 1980 (92.4 percent in 1982) to 73.6 percent by 1988. Nonetheless, Dellums raised $848,795 from individual contributors in 1988, and only $117,458 came in amounts of $500 or more. Dellums, who has claimed to be a man of the people throughout his congressional career, seems to follow this dictum in his fund-raising practices either by intent or by necessity.

The proportion of total contributions consisting of contributions from individuals is related to the topic at hand and bears further consideration. Table 7.6 presents some figures on this proportion.

Nonincumbents relied more heavily on contributions from individuals than did incumbents. Incumbents are generally more experienced in fund-raising than other candidates and are likely to seek funds that are less costly to obtain. Institutional contributors can be assumed to be better informed than individual contributors are, and are aware of the electoral advantage possessed by incumbents; in addition, they are more inclined to support candidates with a clearly defined ideological record than they are to support unknown challengers or open-seat candidates. Individuals certainly supported incumbents with their votes, as the election returns of the eighties show, but some were inclined to take a financial chance on challengers and open-seat candidates. After the incumbent differential is taken into account, there appears to be a consistency between the groups across these election years. For example, early in the decade, blacks relied more heavily on individual contributions than did white male candidates. However, after the 1982 election, this turns around, and in all cases except one, blacks received a smaller percentage of their contributions from individuals than did white male candidates on average.

The differences for women candidates are perhaps the most surprising. In every election women candidates received a larger proportion of their

Table 7.6
Percent of all Contributions Consisting of Individual Contributions
by Status, Race, and Sex

	1980*	1982*	1984	1986	1988
Incumbents					
White Males	55.8%	55.7%	43.8%	43.2%	40.9%
Blacks	60.7%	56.3%	43.6%	34.1%	33.7%
Females	63.2%	57.3%	47.2%	44.9%	46.9%
Nonincumbents					
White Males	70.6%	67.0%	43.8%	49.3%	48.8%
Blacks	81.5%	63.3%	40.1%	56.4%	41.8%
Females	70.9%	69.6%	49.5%	55.1%	56.0%

*The 1980 and 1982 figures include contributions to one's own campaign.

campaign money from individuals than did white male candidates. This applied to both incumbents and nonincumbents. Further, in eight of the ten cases studied, individual contributions made up a larger proportion of women's campaign chests than they did for blacks. This has two implications. First, because individual contributions are more time consuming to raise, valuable campaign time is being absorbed by the need to raise money. Second, if institutional sources of money carry more political baggage as the money/legislation literature suggests, then female candidates as a group may serve with fewer constraints or political IOUs than do their male colleagues.

Individual contributors apparently discriminate against black candidates. This result holds up after electability issues and demographic characteristics are taken into account. On one level the ability to discriminate against black candidates is perfectly legal, if undesirable. However, since individual contributions make up the largest portion of all contributions, a shortfall in this category portends a gloomy future for increasing black representation. Other studies (Derfner 1984, Brace et al. 1988) suggest that black candidates face electability problems unless the district has a large black population. This study provides an additional reason for that result. Black candidates receive lower levels of contributions from individuals in general, although this disadvantage is alleviated to some degree in predominately black districts because the cost of election is often low. Hence, blacks have a more difficult time financing an effective campaign outside districts with large black populations.

Individual contributors are less hostile toward women, although in three cases female candidates did receive significantly lower levels of contributions than did male candidates. Women appear to receive more of their funding from individuals than do either blacks or men. This may lead to fewer constraints on their latitude once elected but at the cost of spending more time on fund-raising activities.

NOTES

1. Prior to 1984, figures were kept differently and cross-year comparisons are less useful. Fortunately the statistical analysis to follow is cross-sectional, and the different accounting methods will not bias our estimates.

2. Under FEC regulations an individual may contribute $1,000 to any one candidate per election (general, primary, and runoff in states with runoff primaries), generally leading to a ceiling of $2,000 per candidate.

3. As discussed previously, there are also individuals who contribute in the expectation of receiving a political return, and that return generates utility. Given that the diffuse objectives of these tit-for-tat contributors defy aggregation, their behavior is indistinguishable from contributors who receive gratification from the contribution act itself. In short, it matters not why people contribute when the reasons are many, but it does matter that they do contribute, how much they contribute, and to whom.

4. There is an upper boundary on individual contributors, imposed by FEC regulations, of $25,000 per year. Politically active and well-to-do people can find ways to circumvent these regulations such as contributing to political action committees and political parties or even making independent expenditures on behalf of or in opposition to a candidate.

5. For a further discussion of demographic traits and political participation that includes additional references see Conway (1991) and Theilmann and Wilhite (1989).

6. Voting and other forms of political participation are also influenced by psychological factors such as a sense of obligation to vote or a strong identification with a political party (Conway 1991).

7. Naturally, some candidates attract contributions from outside their districts, but the bulk of these funds are institutional contributions, coming primarily from PACs. There have been unique instances where a candidate will draw substantial individual contributions from outside his or her district, but these cases are few. For example, in 1982, Dick Durbin (IL 20) attracted many pro-Israel contributions as the incumbent, Paul Findley, had become identified with Palestinian self-determination. While such circumstances would be an interesting topic to pursue, it would lead this study far astray.

Chapter Eight

Money and Representation

It is now time to return to the question of congressional representation of blacks and women. The eighties have been a time of successes as well as unfulfilled aspirations for women and black congressional candidates. Larger numbers of women have run than before, from a low of fifty-three in 1980 to a high of sixty-two in 1986. Well over one-half of the women candidates ran as challengers, except in 1982, when 49 percent ran as challengers and 20 percent ran for open seats. Some of these challengers were well funded. In 1986, the leading female money raiser was a challenger, Kathleen Kennedy Townsend, and in 1988 the three leading female fund-raisers were challengers. Except for Nita Lowey, who captured the New York Twentieth District seat from Rep. Joseph Dio-Guardi in the second-most expensive House race in 1988, the others lost their races.[1] All told, there were six female members of the million dollar club in the 1980s: Cissy Baker (challenger, lost in 1982), Townsend (challenger, lost 1986), Helen Bentley (incumbent, defeated Townsend in 1986), Lowey (challenger, won 1988), Anna Eschoo (challenger, lost 1988), Margaret Mueller (challenger, lost 1988). There were, however, several other women candidates who raised campaign war chests in the $500,000 to $1 million range. Evidently, money was no more of a guarantee of success for female challengers than it was for male challengers.

The situation for black candidates in the 1980s improved as their numbers in Congress increased, but after reaching a peak of thirty-nine black candidates in 1982, their numbers receded thereafter. Once major-

ity black (and substantial minority black) districts gained black representatives, there were few additional blacks running as challengers or for
open seats. Black incumbents generally did better than national norms,
handily winning reelection with vote totals averaging 83 percent in 1986
and 85 percent in 1988. In some cases black challengers ran against black
incumbents, although to no avail. Black candidates did not run as
expensive races as did women candidates. Only Ron Dellums exceeded
the $1 million mark in 1986 and 1988. Some other black incumbents
were still winning races in 1986 and 1988 with spending totals less than
$250,000.

THE IMPACT OF MONEY ON THE ELECTION OF
WOMEN AND BLACKS

Based on our empirical results, several interesting and often unexpected funding differentials appear. Black candidates received less
funding than did white candidates, in the range of $7,000 to almost
$30,000 less through the 1980s. On the other hand, aggregate funding
received by women candidates was not significantly different from that
received by male candidates.

Additional discrepencies arose when different sources of contributions
were studied. For example, PACs displayed a tendency to discriminate
on the basis of race and sex, but the direction of this differential depended
on candidate status. Black incumbents typically received less money than
did white incumbents when a differential existed. The dominant case
involved trade, membership, and health PACs, which gave between
$8,000 and $15,000 less to black incumbents in four of the five elections
studied. Conversely, nonincumbent blacks were often helped by PAC
contributions, most notably by labor and nonaligned PACs.

PAC contributions to female incumbents were typically indistinguishable from contributions to incumbent men, providing little evidence of
discrimination. Nonincumbent female candidates appeared to benefit
from PAC contributions as most of the differentials were positive.
Particularly prominent were the nonaligned PAC contributions, which
totaled between $4,700 and $8,200 more to women candidates in four
of the five elections.

Political parties acted to increase the number of successful minority
candidates. While there were few instances in which a political party based
contributions to incumbents on gender or color, contributions to nonincumbents often favored blacks and women. The Democratic party
appears to have funneled money to black challengers in three of the five

elections. The Republican party was not as aggressive (not fielding black candidates in 1988) in the race dimension, although they contributed significantly greater funds to female candidates in two of the five elections.

Overall, individual contributors displayed little racial or sexual delineation in either the incumbent and nonincumbent regressions. When large individual contributions (those greater than $500) are singled out, black candidates received significantly less money in half of the campaigns studied.

While several theoretical and empirical questions have been addressed in the course of this study, the focus has been a broadly defined single issue: direct sexual or racial discrimination. Specifically, if two candidates are indistinguishable in terms of electability and ideology, are the contributions they receive affected by their race and/or gender? While information on this direct discrimination is central, it is not the complete tale. Operating in addition to direct discrimination is the possibility of indirect discrimination. Indirect discrimination is a two-step process. First, we recognize the possibility that some candidates may be treated differently because they share a common characteristic other than race or gender that affects their contributions. If a disproportionate share of a minority happens to be represented in one of these categories, they will suffer disproportionately. In employment law this circumstance is called "disparate impact" and is recognized in the courts as an actionable grievance. For example, suppose promotion in a law firm is primarily determined by senority. Because blacks and women are relative newcomers to this profession, this promotion rule is said to have a "disparate impact" on blacks and women. Unless the firm can establish some business reason for this policy, the firm can be charged with discrimination.

In the world of congressional campaigns, incumbency plays a dominant role. Scholars have recognized the incumbency advantage for years, and recently the issue has occupied a growing portion of the general public's attention. While it has been noted (Baxter and Lansing 1983, Bernstein 1986, Darcy, Welch, and Clark 1987) that black and women candidates face an incumbency dilemma, measurement of its impact is rare. In the 1980s, 57.8 percent of the women running for Congress were challengers and 10.4 percent were open-seat candidates, while 31.7 percent of the black candidates were challengers and 7.6 percent ran for open seats. Because challengers face increased difficulties raising campaign funds, it appears that women candidates are at a particular disadvantage.

An impression of the magnitude of a disparate opportunity due to incumbency differences can be discerned by eliminating information about candidates' status as incumbents or challengers and reestimating our models of contributions. These estimated parameters can then be used to calculate a "total impact" of race/sex and incumbency. A disparate impact will then be reflected in the difference between the direct effect of race and sex and the total effect after incumbency status has been included.

Calculating these total impacts we found that black and female candidates suffer indirect discrimination, but the largest indirect effects were in PAC contributions. Indirect effects were practically absent in individual and party contributions. There is an intuitive sense to this finding because PACs represent special-interest groups who are interested in gaining the ear of a representative. This objective renders contributions to losers useless, something PACs want to avoid. Individuals, however, are viewed as participating in the campaign process partially because they gain utility from the participation. Candidate status is less important than are other motivations for many individual contributors.

The lack of an indirect effect for political parties was more disconcerting. This behavior is incongruent with a strategy of obtaining or maintaining a majority in Congress, but it is consistent with the empirical results that implied parties are trying to increase minority representation. A policy directing contributions toward blacks and women should be less concerned with candidate status.

Because the PAC results reflect significant differences between direct and indirect effects, they warrant closer scrutiny. Table 8.1 reports the estimated direct and indirect effects of race and sex on PAC contributions but omits estimated coefficients of all the other explanatory variables used in the preceding chapters. Those variables are of less interest because they are similar to previous estimates or they reflect the impact of both incumbents and nonincumbents, which muddles interpretation.[2] For this reason, Table 8.1 consists exclusively of direct and total funding differentials.

Including the possibility of a disparate impact increases the number of cases of significant statistical sexual and/or racial discrimination. This increase is particularly acute for women candidates. For blacks the disparate impact of discrimination offsets the direct impact, leaving the total effect unchanged. In 1988, trade, membership, and health PACs, for example, were found to directly discriminate against black candidates by $15,000. When we remember that most black candidates in 1988 were incumbents, the total impact disappears. If the goal is one of no racial or sexual response, we should be hesitant to accept this zero-total impact as an accomplishment of that goal. If in the aggregate there is no evidence

Table 8.1
Direct and Total Impacts of Race and Sex

	1980	1982	1984	1986	1988
BLACK CANDIDATES					
Labor PACs					
direct	$1000	$7700	----	$12,000	----
total	$6200	----	$7000	$21,000	$24,000
Corporate PACs					
direct	$8500	----	----	----	-$16,000
total	----	-$13,000	----	----	----
Trade, Membership and Health PACs					
direct	-$3900	-$10,800	-$12,000	----	-$15,000
total	----	-$9900	----	----	----
Cooperative PACs					
direct	----	-$2800	-$1900	----	----
total	----	-$3600	-$2400	----	----
Nonaligned PACs					
direct	----	----	----	$19,000	$14,000
total	----	----	----	$11,000	$13,000
FEMALE CANDIDATES					
Labor PACs					
direct	----	-$9500	$3.900	----	----
total	----	----	----	----	----
Corporate PACs					
direct	----	----	----	----	----
total	-$10,000	----	-$13,500	-$15,500	-$2200
Trade, Membership and Health PACs					
direct	$3200	----	$2800	----	----
total	----	-$4600	----	-$8500	----
Cooperative PACs					
direct	-$1100	-$1600	-$600	----	-$400
total	-$2600	-$1700	----	-$2000	-$1800
Nonaligned PACs					
direct	$2300	$3000	$3500	----	$3600
indirect	----	$3100	----	----	----

The direct effect equals the impact for incumbents or nonincumbents, whichever is significant, their average if both are significant, and a blank when neither is significant.

of antiblack sentiment simply because a few successful black representatives have advantages that overwhelm the aggregate results, this will
be a situation ripe for backsliding. With the retirement of a successful
incumbent, that statistically positive factor is removed and the negative
direct effect will once again dominate. Eradication of statistical racial or
sexual discrimination can only be called complete when both the direct
and indirect effects are independently zero.

The bottom half of Table 8.1 gives the female contribution differentials
for PACs when candidate status is included (the direct effect) and when
status is eliminated (the total effect). A quick glance shows female
candidates are generally worse off when indirect discrimination is
considered. Chapter 5 demonstrated that there was no evidence of direct
discrimination by corporate PACs on the basis of sex. When the total
effect is estimated, there are statistically significant sexual differentials
in four of the five election cycles. Including women challengers reveals
that corporate PACs contributed between $2,000 and $15,000 less to
female candidates in the 1980s. Trade, membership, and health PACs
had a negative total female differential in 1982 and 1986, even though
the direct effects in those years were indistinguishable from zero.
Cooperatives' PACs had a direct negative impact on women candidates
in the range of $400 to $1,600, but including the indirect impact the
differentials rose to a range of $1,700 to $2,600.

An important caveat—measurement of the total effect—helps our
understanding of the underrepresentation of blacks and women in Congress, but it is not necessarily the case that this "discrimination" is
racially or sexually motivated. While corporate PACs contribute less
money to female candidates, their reason may well be because fewer
women are incumbents. PACs, as we have learned, are centrally interested in congressional lobbying, and successful candidates are a necessary condition for the achievement of this objective. It would be
inappropriate to suggest corporate PACs are operating in a manner
designed to eliminate female and black candidates simply because the
total effects suggest less funding.[3]

Even if total funding differentials are only coincidentally related to
race and sex, they impose a burden on the candidate. Candidates facing
difficulty raising money from institutional sources will have a more
difficult time winning elections. Hence, racial and sexual contribution
differentials will have an impact on election results and in the long run
on the composition of Congress, regardless of the intent of the contributor. Although we cannot know the origin of the inequity, the current

state of campaign financing suggests further sexual and racial integration of Congress will be an arduous task.

RENT SEEKING IN POLITICS

Chapter 4 introduced a theoretical approach to political campaigns based on rent-seeking, the pursuit of a valuable prize through a contest imposing costs on the participants and society. This approach allowed us rigorously to structure objective functions for candidates and contributors that, in turn, generated hypotheses suitable for empirical testing. Starting with mild assumptions such as rationality and self-interest, we explored strategies and decisions of a wide variety of individuals. When we factor in the substantial disadvantages faced by challengers and add the information that 95 percent or more of the incumbents win re-election, legitimate questions arise such as: Why does anyone run as a challenger? and similarly, are these challengers rational?

Our model does not attempt to measure all aspects of candidate decision making (such an attempt is doomed at the outset), but a decision to run as a challenger falls in a set of logical solutions. Our model suggests several reasons why running as a challenger might be optimal behavior for some people. First, candidates generally act on the basis of an expected return. Even if the probability of winning is quite small, when weighted by the large return, a positive expected return may apply to the longest of longshots and provide sufficient encouragement for a challenger to make the effort. The expected return need only outweigh the expected cost for candidates' decisions to be "rational." Second, a large portion of campaign costs come from third parties, not from the candidate. A candidate can initiate a mild, almost exploratory campaign, and if it seems to be successful, generating interest and money, she can increase her involvement without putting all of her personal resources in jeopardy. Third, the decision to run for a congressional seat is typically made months before election day. With the election a year away, it is not always clear that the incumbent has a lock on a seat. Incumbents are unseated every election, and a challenger has to be in place to pick off one of these plums. Fourth, while the dominant return of a congressional election is the occupation of a seat, it is not the exclusive return. Some candidates run to gain name recognition, to enhance their standing in the party, and to establish a base for another election. Many successful challengers win after their second or third onslaught on an incumbent.

The model serves equally well in its dissection of incumbent behavior. A question that is rarely asked is, why do incumbents bother to mount a re-election campaign? This seemingly silly conjecture is logically identical to the oft-questioned motives of challengers. If incumbents have a palpable advantage and more than 95 percent of them are re-elected, how can the expenditure of millions of dollars be rational? Our answer to this question is a reciprocal to challengers' motives. An incumbent has a lot to lose, so even with a small probability of loss the potential is significant; third parties bear much of the financial burden; and re-election may not appear predestined a year in advance. Recognizing that incumbents and challengers are essentially facing the same decision under different probabilities makes their actions logical.

Open-seat elections have candidates facing the same decision, but now both players have preelection probabilities of success that are much closer to one another. It directly follows that candidates will be attracted to these elections, and campaigning will be furious.

Few of these conclusions are unique, although our theory does challenge some conventions; for example, challengers are responsive to incumbents expenditures unlike some claims (e.g., Jacobson 1980, 1985, Ragsdale and Cook 1987). However, what is unique is the existence of a single approach that generates all of these results. Further, the rent-seeking model applies to contributors as well as to candidates. Contributors realize candidates face constraints, and while their contributions may be appreciated the return they can expect to receive will be tempered by the influence of the candidates' other supporters, personal ideology, probability of winning the election, and their congressional clout. Contributors adopt strategies similar to any investment decision by balancing the expected returns of contributions to one candidate against the contributions to another and against other investment opportunities.

Our analysis has given an indication that financial hurdles exist for female and black candidates, although they may not be of the size casual observation might suggest. The acquisition of additional seats may be slow in coming. While measuring this financial gap is the intended goal of this work, an underlying question remains. How does this situation affect the representation of blacks and women? Although this deeper question lies beyond our immediate grasp, our theoretical construct and empirical results enable us to peer further into the gloom.

REPRESENTATION

Is there any reason to be concerned with the number of black and female representatives? The answer to this question depends on our concept of representation. If the political process is capable of judging representative abilities, society is certainly better off if all its citizens are potential candidates for Congress. With a larger pool of possible candidates there is more talent available to enter Congress. Accepting that position, does the resulting composition of Congress matter?

In chapter 1 we defined two types of representation: descriptive, in which the demographic composition of Congress reflects the population of the district or the nation at large; and substantive, in which the issues of concern to blacks and women are given their due in the deliberations of Congress. If solely the first definition is adopted, increased numbers of blacks and women as well as other minority groups must be elected to the House and Senate. The number of black representatives will have to roughly triple, and close to 200 men would have to be replaced by women. Obviously the incumbency bias and the saturation of black majority districts will push this goal into the distant future.

If, on the other hand, achieving substantive representation is our goal, there may be no need for any representatives actually to be black or female. All that is necessary is for the political system to be responsive to the wishes of its constituents and effective lines of communication to be established.

The current situation is somewhere between these extremes. It seems unlikely that total descriptive representation is required to achieve substantive representation, but substantive representation is probably enhanced by some degree of literal, descriptive representation. Different backgrounds and cultural surroundings produce people who think differently and have different values. Their insights and imagination can be beneficial to the whole in the lawmaking process.

A convincing argument can be made that some issues shared by blacks, women, or other minorities are more convincingly presented and defended by people of that group. This perspective argues for demographic representation. Further, given that Congress is a democratic body, a single member or simply a few members of a large constituent group may not provide adequate representation. There is likely some "critical mass" necessary to bring issues before the House with sufficient force to guarantee consideration. The number of representatives necessary to achieve this critical mass is unknown and probably differs from issue to issue, but it is difficult to imagine that it is only met with complete descriptive representation.

Does the election of women and blacks to Congress force male congressmen to change their stance on issues and become more responsive to their constituents? Does the election of women and blacks to

Congress help to provide further evidence for the existence of a democratizing trend that had started in the nineteenth century and has opened the political process to all Americans to participate in any fashion? If the answer to either set of questions is in the affirmative, then achieving some measure of descriptive representation for women and blacks is important. This goal of descriptive representation should also be important to at least some institutional contributors who can be assumed to have a stake in the preservation of a democratic electoral system. Political parties, at least, seem to have tried somewhat to achieve the goal of descriptive representation through their campaign contributions.

The goal of achieving demographic parity for women and blacks in Congress is a simplistic solution that largely ignores the implications of representation. Nonetheless, providing a situation in which blacks and women have a better chance to gain election to Congress than presently exists, even if not achieving numbers exactly equal to their proportion of the U.S. population, may make Congress more reflective of social wishes.

WHERE DO WE GO FROM HERE?

There are many constraints on the number of women and blacks in Congress. The most important is the tendency of U.S. voters to criticize Congress and then reelect their own representatives. Darcy, Welch, and Clark (1987) estimate that because of incumbency, women will not achieve representation in Congress equal to their share of the population until well into the twenty-first century. Achieving representation for blacks equal to their share of the population will likely take as long. As indicated above, numbers are not the total story. Congress is more responsive to the concerns of black and female Americans than it was twenty years ago. This responsiveness may be due to increased constituent demands, but it seems likely that the growing numbers of black and female representatives deserve some of the credit. What is also evident is that neither group is monolithic, with all women and blacks sharing the same concerns. This trend toward a diversity of goals will likely continue in the nineties. The 1990 election brought the first black Republican representative to Congress since 1935, Gary Franks (CT 5).

Achieving a higher level of representation for blacks and women is possible, but overcoming the incumbency bias will be difficult. One often-cited panacea is some sort of term limitation for Congress. Such a solution is certainly attractive if weakening the incumbency bias is the sole goal. Unfortunately this solution is fraught with other problems such as removing able legislators from Congress. Another alternative involves the unlikely option of increasing the number of congressional districts.

Another less-harsh solution would be to make congressional elections more competitive for female and black candidates, and financial resources can help. Not all big-spending challengers can overcome incumbents' advantages, but there may be a spending threshold they must surpass in order to be competitive (Jacobson 1987). Big-spending races also increase turnout (Gilliam 1985, Caldiera, Patterson, and Markko 1985), which in turn makes for a more competitive race. Two problems are apparent. Without limiting total spending or incumbent spending, such a solution is likely to drive up further the costs of elections. Achieving challenger financial parity with incumbents will be difficult to accomplish, particularly since few incumbents are likely to vote for any changes in the present system of campaign finance that would decrease their chances for reelection. Changing contributor attitudes, especially PAC views of black candidates, may provide some benefit, but PACs play the current game quite well. There is little return in their adoption of an altruistic goal.

The political environment for black congressional candidates changed profoundly in the 1980s, and the horizon for the 1990s is different still. In 1980, 43 percent of black congressional candidates were challengers, and several districts with large black populations had white representatives. In the 1988 election the situation was completely different. Almost all of the black congressional candidates were incumbents; only Faye Williams ran as a challenger to Clyde Holloway (LA 8). Most of these representatives came from districts with substantial black populations, and only one majority black district remained represented by a white representative (this district, LA 2, elected William Jefferson in 1990, completing the set of black districts electing black representatives).

These black incumbents appear to be quite secure and adept at raising money for future campaigns. Because they often run in "safe" districts, black incumbents are less driven by a need to raise money than are some other candidates. It is probably safe to predict that these seats will usually be filled by minority candidates in the future, but that does not rule out the possibility that a few of these seats could switch from black to Hispanic representatives. After the 1990 election a total of twenty-six black representatives could be found in Congress (one was the nonvoting representative from Washington, D.C.), two more than in 1988. This historic high includes one Republican and three additional black women: Barbara Rose-Collins (MI 13), Maxine Waters (CA 29), and Eleanor Holmes-Norton (Washington, D.C.).[4]

Further growth in the number of black representatives will probably be increasingly difficult. Redistricting in the wake of the 1990 census is likely to create a few additional black majority districts in the South in 1992. Beyond these potential new seats, black candidates face the incumbent advantage and often less funding than do their white counterparts. How can black candidates become more competitive in districts with few black voters? Such races, whether contested as challengers or open-seat candidates, are likely to be more expensive than running in a black majority district, so once again the ability to attract campaign funds is important. In essence, black candidates running in white-majority districts try to turn out black voters and still attract white voters by reassuring them. This strategy will be difficult to carry out; as the results of the 1990 North Carolina Senate race suggest, antiblack sentiments persist as they helped to tip the balance against Harvey Gantt in his challenge to Jesse Helms. The complexity of attracting both black and white voters requires black candidates to raise greater financial resources than comparable white candidates. Will black candidates running in white-majority districts be able to achieve the financial resources necessary to be competitive? Our research suggests it will be difficult to accomplish. If this is true, there seems to be a built-in limit to the number of blacks who will be elected to Congress.

Women candidates seem to be at less of a financial disadvantage. Their success works for and against them. Voters no longer see women as novelties, and so, with the possible exception of voters in the South, consider them from perspectives other than gender. Women candidates thus do not seem to have a built-in constituency to build upon. Conversely, there seems to be less residual opposition to the election of women to public office. Nonetheless, gains for women seem to be slowing. Voters elected thirty-one women to Congress in 1990 (twenty-nine in the House and two in the Senate) which is four more than were elected in 1988, but, because of the special election victories of four women in the interim, only equalled the number present when Congress adjourned in 1990. The funding picture seems to bear out this twin perspective. Women candidates fare no better nor no worse than do their male counterparts of comparable status when it comes to obtaining financial resources. This situation is an improvement over their financial position in the seventies, but superior financial resources would certainly help women increase their numbers in Congress.

The prospect for women and blacks has improved since the early years of the Republic. Women and blacks participate in the political arena far more widely today than they did at any time in the past. They are coming closer to participating as equals with white males when it comes to running for office. Obviously we are a long way from being a society in which only substantive representation matters, a society in which a white woman could represent a black majority district or a black male represent a largely white and Hispanic district without either situation arousing comment. Achieving partial descriptive representation promotes substantive representation, but that first goal remains distant.

Campaign resources are not the only determinant affecting changes, but they are an important piece of the puzzle. As we have shown, the funding picture for black and female candidates has improved during the eighties, an improvement that has enhanced their electability. Further improvements will be more difficult to achieve in the nineties. But, if contributors are indeed rent-seekers, they will provide at least equal funding for black and female candidates, other things being equal. Even though this will not markedly improve the chances of black and female challengers, the threat of change might cause some white male candidates to become more responsive to their female and black constituents.

Changing how we elect our representatives or how we finance congressional elections will have an impact on the composition and actions of Congress. Changes that are made should be made with care if Congress is to reflect the views of all Americans.

NOTES

1. Even so, it took the the aid of Lowey's friend and former neighbor, Mario Cuomo, to pull off the upset.

2. For example, when LASTVOTE was included in an incumbent and a non-incumbent equation it was expected to be positive in one and negative in the other. Combining the samples will move the estimate towards zero and insignificance.

3. If this was a legal case, the disparate impact from corporate PAC contributions could be readily defended as having a "business" justification, and so the suit would probably be thrown out.

4. Rose-Collins succeeded George Crockett, who retired. Waters succeeded Augustus Hawkins, who retired. Holmes-Norton succeeded Walter Fauntroy, who resigned to run for mayor of Washington, D.C. Hence, the two-seat gain for blacks in Congress came with Gary Franks of Connecticut and William Jefferson of Louisiana.

Appendix: Data and Variable Definitions

DATA SOURCES

Most of our data comes from data tapes contained in the *Report of Financial Activity, Senate and House, 1979–1980, 1981–1982, 1983–1984, 1985–1986,* and *1987–1988* prepared by the Federal Election Commission. These reports give information on campaign contributions for every candidate for the House and Senate. In addition to total contributions there are subcategories such as PAC contributions (also broken into various types of PACs) (chapter 5), major political party contributions (chapter 6), and contributions by individuals (chapter 7). Also included on this tape are election data (vote percentages), and geographical locations (the district and state of the candidates).

As part of the exploration of the trade-off of votes and money, information on a number of other factors is also necessary. Candidates' race and sex as well as their voting records are of concern. Most of this data was obtained from Alan Ehrenhalt, ed., *Politics in America, 1980, 1982, 1984, 1986, 1988* (Washington, D.C.: CQ Press, 1981, 1983, 1985, 1987); Phil Duncan, ed., *Politics in America, 1990* (Washington, D.C.: CQ Press, 1989); and various issues of *Congressional Quarterly Weekly Reports*. Some constituent characteristics and interests and demographic characteristics of congressional districts are important. This information is collected from *Congressional Districts in the 1970s and 1980s* (Washington, D.C.: CQ Press, 1972, 1983).

MNEMONICS AND VARIABLE DEFINITIONS

AFL: A two-year average of the AFL-CIO rating of voting records of members of Congress.

AGEPOP: Median age of the population in each congressional district.

BLACK: A dummy variable set equal to one for black candidates, equal to zero for nonblacks.

BLACKPOP: Percentage of the population in each congressional district consisting of blacks.

CCUS: A two-year average of the U.S. Chamber of Congress's ratings of voting records of members of Congress.

COMMITTEE: A dummy variable set equal to one for representatives who chair or are the ranking minority member of a House standing committee. Also coded one are the Speaker of the House, majority and minority leaders, and Democratic and Republican whips. These representatives are likely to be the most influential members of the House.

CONTRIBUTION$: Consists of total campaign contributions received by a candidate in the current election cycle. Measured in thousands of dollars.

COOP$: Contributions to candidates by nonparty political action committees reporting a connection to a cooperative. This category is delineated by the FEC.

CORP$: Contributions to candidates by nonparty political action committees reporting a connection to a corporation. This category is delineated by the FEC.

DEMOCRAT: A dummy variable set equal to one for candidates who are members of the Democratic party.

EDUCPOP: Median years of school attained by the population in each congressional district.

FEMALE: A dummy variable set equal to one for female candidates.

INCOMPOP: Median income of the population in each congressional district.

INCUMB: A dummy variable set equal to one for candidates who are incumbents. All other candidates are coded with a zero.

INDIV$: Contributions to candidates from individuals. This category is delineated by the FEC.

LABOR$: Contributions to candidates by nonparty political action committees reporting a connection to organized labor. This category is delineated by the FEC.

LASTVOTE: The percentage of the vote received by the candidate in the previous election (expressed as a decimal). Challengers and candidates for open seats, of course, may lack previous vote percentage. In those cases the vote percentage received by the candidate's party in the previous election is used as a proxy. It then reflects only a portion of the candidate strength, that is, the strength of party affiliation in the district.

NONALIGN$: Contributions to candidates by nonparty political action committees that have not reported a connected organization. This category is delineated by the FEC.

OPEN: A dummy variable set equal to one for candidates involved in races with no incumbent. All other candidates coded as zero.

OPPONENT$: Measures the opponent's total campaign contributions in thousands of dollars.

PARTY$: Contributions to candidates plus expenditures on behalf of candidates by one of the major political parties. This category is delineated by the FEC.

PU: A two-year average of the annual party unity index calculated by *Congressional Quarterly*.

RATIO$: The ratio of the candidate's spending relative to spending by both candidates. Explicitly for candidates X and Y: RATIO$X = SPEND$X/(SPEND$X + SPEND$Y).

SPEND$: Total campaign expenditures by a candidate, measured in thousands of dollars.

TENURE: The number of years incumbent candidates have been in the House.

TENURE^2: The square of TENURE, indicative of the declining marginal return of tenure in the House.

TRADE$: Contributions to candidates by nonparty political action committees reporting a connection to a trade association or a membership organization or from committees in health-related areas. This category is delineated by the FEC.

%VOTE: The percentage of the vote received by a candidate in the current election. Expressed as decimals, for instance, $10\% = .1$

VOTEGAP: Set equal to the absolute value of $(X - .5)$, where X is the candidate's proportion of the vote in the election. The absolute value is taken to equate the situations of losing by x percent and winning by x percent. In every election one candidate wins and the other loses, but this variable indicates the closeness of the race. As an election becomes increasingly lopsided, the value of VOTEGAP increases, while a dead heat would produce a VOTEGAP equal to zero. More explicitly, notice the difference between VOTEGAP and %VOTE. Suppose a candidate won the previous election with 85 percent of the vote. His %VOTE value is .85, indicating a strong candidate, and the challenger's %VOTE is .15, indicating a weak candidate. However, *both* candidates have a VOTEGAP measure of .35, indicating that the current race is probably not too exciting. In chapter 4 the square is used instead on the absolute value to identify the system.

Bibliography

Abney, F. Glenn. 1974. "Factors Related to Negro Turnout in Mississippi." *Journal of Politics* 37: 1057–63.

Abramson, Paul R. 1983. *Political Participation in America*. San Francisco: W. H. Freeman.

Abramson, Paul R., and William H. Claggett. 1984. "Race-Related Differences in Self-Reported and Validated Turnout." *Journal of Politics* 46: 719–38.

Adamany, David, and George F. Agree. 1975. *Political Money: A Strategy for Campaign Financing in America*. Baltimore: Johns Hopkins University Press.

Aldrich, John R. 1983a. "A Downsian Spatial Model with Party Activism." *American Political Science Review* 77: 974–90.

———. 1983b. "A Spatial Model with Party Activists: Implications for Electoral Dynamics." *Public Choice* 41: 63–100.

Alexander, Herbert E. 1984. *Financing Politics*. 3d ed. Washington, D.C.: CQ Press.

Amemiya, Takeshi. 1973. "Regression Analysis When the Dependent Variable is Truncated Normal." *Econometrica* 41: 997–1016.

Ball, Howard, Dale Kane, and Thomas P. Lauth. 1982. *Congressional Compliance: Implementation of the 1965 Voting Rights Act*. Westport, Conn.: Greenwood Press.

Barnett, Marguerite Ross. 1982. "The Congressional Black Caucus: Illusions and Realities of Power." In *The New Black Politics*, ed. M. B. Preston, L. J. Henderson, Jr. and P. Puryer, pp. 28–54. New York: Longman.

Baxter, Sandra, and Marjorie Lansing. 1983. *Women and Politics*. Rev. ed. Ann Arbor: University of Michigan Press.

Beiler, David. 1990. "How to Defeat Women and Blacks." *Campaigns & Elections* 11 (August/September): 52–54.

Bender, Bruce. 1986. "The Determinants of Relative Political Campaign Expenditures." *Economic Inquiry* 24: 231–256.

Bernstein, Robert A. 1986. "Why Are there so Few Women in the House?" *Western Political Quarterly* 39: 155–164.

Black, Earl, and Merle Black. 1987. *Politics and Society in the South.* Cambridge, Mass.: Harvard University Press.

Bobo, Lawrence, and Franklin D. Gilliam, Jr. 1990. "Race, Sociopolitical Participation, and Black Empowerment." *American Political Science Review* 84: 377–93.

Brace, Kimball, Bernard N. Grofman, Lisa R. Handley, and Richard G. Niemi. 1988. "Minority Voting Equality: The 65 Percent Rule in Theory and Practice." *Law and Policy* 10: 43–62.

Brauer, Carl. 1983. "Women Activists, Southern Conservatives, and the Prohibition of Sex Discrimination in Title VII of the 1964 Civil Rights Act." *Journal of Southern History* 49: 37–56.

Brennan, Geoffrey, and James Buchanan. 1984. "Voter Choice." *American Behavioral Scientist* 28: 185–201.

Bullock, Charles S., III. 1981. "Congressional Voting and the Mobilization of a Black Electorate in the South." *Journal of Politics* 43: 662–682.

Burke, Edmund. 1948. "Speech to the Electors of Bristol at the Conclusion of the poll, 3 November 1774." In *Selected Prose of Edmund Burke*, ed. Philip Magnus. London: Falcon Press.

Burrell, Barbara C. 1986. "Women's and Men's Campaigns for the U.S. House of Representatives, 1972–1982, A Finance Gap?" *American Politics Quarterly* 13: 251–72.

Caldeira, Gregory A., Samuel C. Patterson, and Gregory A. Markko. 1985. "The Mobilization of Voters in Congressional Elections." *Journal of Politics* 47: 490–509.

Carroll, Susan J. 1985. *Women as Candidates in American Politics.* Bloomington: Indiana University Press.

Carson, Richard T., and Joe A. Oppenheimer. 1984. "A Method of Estimating the Personal Ideology of Political Representatives." *American Political Science Review* 78: 163–78.

Chappell, Henry W. 1982. "Campaign Contributions and Congressional Voting: A Simultaneous Probit-Tobit Model." *Review of Economics and Statistics* 61: 77–83.

Chappell, Henry W., and William R. Keech. 1986. "Policy Motivation and Party Differences in a Dynamic Spatial Model of Party Competition." *American Political Science Review* 80: 881–99.

Christopher, Maurine. 1976. *Black Americans in Congress.* Rev. ed. New York: Thomas Y. Crowell.

Clausen, Aage R. 1973. *How Congressmen Decide: A Policy Focus.* New York: St. Martin's Press.

Clausen, Aage R., and Carl E. Van Horn. 1977. "The Congressional Response to a Decade of Change: 1963–1972." *Journal of Politics* 39: 624–66.

Combs, Michael W., John R. Hibbing, and Susan Welch. 1984. "Black Constituents and Role Call Votes." *Western Political Quarterly* 37: 424–34.

Conlon, Richard P. 1987. "The Declining Importance of Individual Contributions in Financing Congressional Campaigns." *Journal of Law and Politics* 3: 467–98.

Conway, M. Margaret. 1991. *Political Participation in the United States*. 2nd ed. Washington, D.C.: CQ Press.

_____. 1986. "PACs and Congressional Elections in the 1980s." In *Interest Groups Politics*, ed. Allan J. Cigler and Burdett A. Loomis, 2d ed., pp. 70–90. Washington, D.C.: CQ Press.

Crain, Mark, and Robert D. Tollison. 1976. "Campaign Expenditures and Political Competition." *Journal of Law and Economics* 19: 177–188.

Crain, Mark, William F. Shugart II, and Robert D. Tollison. 1988. "Voters as Investors: A Rent-Seeking Resolution to the Paradox of Voting." In *The Political Economy of Rent Seeking*, ed. Charles Rowley, Robert Tollison, and Gordon Tullock, pp. 104–32. Boston: Kluwer Academic Publishers.

Crotty, William J., and Gary C. Jacobson. 1980. *American Parties in Decline*. Boston: Little Brown and Co.

Darcy, Robert, and Sarah Slavin Schramm. 1977. "When Women Run Against Men." *Public Opinion Quarterly* 41: 1–12.

Darcy, Robert, and James R. Choike. 1986. "A Formal Analysis of Legislative Turnover: Women Candidates and Legislative Representation." *American Journal of Political Science* 30: 237–55.

Darcy, Robert, Susan Welch, and Janet Clarke. 1987. *Women, Elections, and Representation*. New York: Longman.

Darcy, Robert, and Charles Hadley. 1988. "Black Women in Politics: The Puzzle of Success." *Social Science Quarterly* 69: 629–45.

Darden, Joe T. 1984. "Black Political Underrepresentation in Majority Black Places." *Journal of Black Studies* 15: 101–16.

Days, Drew S. III, and Lani Guinier. 1984. "Enforcement of Section 5 of the Voting Rights Act." In *Minority Vote Dilution*, ed. Chandler Davidson, pp. 167–80. Washington, D.C.: Howard University Press.

Derfner, Armand. 1984. "Vote Dilution and the Voting Rights Act Amendments of 1982." In *Minority Vote Dilution*, pp. 145–67.

Diamond, Irene. 1977. *Sex Roles in the State House*. New Haven: Yale University Press.

Dobra, John L., and William Lee Eubank. 1985. "Political Survivorship: An Interest Group Perspective." *Southern Economic Journal* 51: 1038–52.

Downs, Anthony. 1957. *An Economic Theory of Democracy*. New York: Harper and Row.

Drew, Elizabeth. 1983. *Politics and Money*. New York: Collier Books.

DuBois, Ellen C. 1978. *Feminism and Suffrage: The Emergence of an Independent Women's Movement in America, 1818–1869*. Ithaca: Cornell University Press.

Duncan, Phil, ed. 1989. *Politics in America, 1990*. Washington, D.C.: CQ Press.

Ehrenhalt, Alan, ed. 1987. *Politics in America, The 100th Congress*. Washington, D.C.: CQ Press.

Eismeier, Theodore J., and Philip H. Pollock III. 1985. "An Organizational Analysis of Political Action Committees." *Political Behavior* 7: 192–216.

_____. 1986a. "Politics and Markets: Corporate Money in American National Elections." *British Journal of Political Science* 16: 287–309.

_____. 1986b. "Strategy and Choice in Congressional Elections: the Role of Political Action Committees." *American Journal of Political Science* 30: 197–213.

_____. 1988. *Business, Money and the Rise of Corporate PACs*. Westport, Conn.: Greenwood Press.

Engstrom, Richard L., and John K. Wildgen. 1977. "Pruning Thorns from the Thicket: An Empirical Test of the Existence of Racial Gerrymandering." *Legislative Studies Quarterly* 2: 465-79.

Enlow, James M., and Melvin J. Hinich. 1984. *The Spatial Theory of Voting*. Cambridge: Cambridge University Press.

Etzioni, Amitai. 1984. *Capital Corruption*. New York: Harcourt Brace.

Eulau, Heinz, and Paul D. Karps. 1977. "The Puzzle of Representation: Specifying Components of Responsiveness." *Legislative Studies Quarterly* 2: 233-54.

Evans, Diana. 1988. "Oil PACs and Aggresive Contribution Strategies." *Journal of Politics* 50: 1047-56.

Evans, Sara. 1979. *Personal Politics*. New York: Knopf.

Fenno, Richard F., Jr. 1973. *Congressmen in Committees*. Boston: Little Brown.

_____. 1978. *Home Style: House Members in Their Own Districts*. Boston: Little Brown.

Fowler, Linda L., and Robert D. McClure. 1989. *Political Ambition: Who Decides to Run for Congress*. New Haven: Yale University Press.

Fowlkes, Diane. 1984. "Ambitious Political Woman: Countersocialization and Political Party Context." *Women & Politics* 4: 5-32.

Gertzog, Irwin N. 1984. *Congressional Women: Their Recruitment, Treatment, and Behavior*. New York: Praeger.

Gilliam, Franklin D., Jr. 1985. "Influences on Voter Turnout for U. S. House Elections in Nonpresidential Years." *Legislative Studies Quarterly* 10: 339-51.

Godwin, R. Kenneth. 1988. *One Billion Dollars of Influence*. Chatham, N.J.: Chatham House.

Goldenberg, Edie, and Michael W. Traugott. 1984. *Campaigning for Congress*. Washington, D.C.: CQ Press.

Gopoian, J. David. 1984. "What Makes PACs Tick? An Analysis of the Allocation Patterns of Economic Interest Groups." *American Journal of Political Science* 28: 259-81.

Green, Donald P., and Jonathan S. Krasno. 1988. "Salvation for the Spendthrift Incumbents: Reestimating the Effects of Campaign Spending in House Elections." *American Journal of Political Science* 32: 884-907.

_____. 1990. "Rebuttal to Jacobson's 'New Evidence for Old Arguments,' " *American Journal of Political Science* 34: 360-72.

Grenzke, Janet M. 1989a. "Candidate Attributes and PAC Contributions." *Western Political Quarterly* 42: 245-64.

_____. 1989b. "PACs and the Congressional Supermarket: the Currency is Complex." *American Journal of Political Science,* 33: 1-24.

Grimes, Alan P. 1967. *The Puritan Ethic and Woman Suffrage*. New York: Oxford University Press.

Hain, Paul. 1974. "Age, Ambition, and Political Careers: The Middle-Age Crisis." *Western Political Quarterly* 27: 265-74.

Hardin, Russell. 1982. *Collective Action*. Baltimore: Johns Hopkins University Press.

Harrison, Cynthia E. 1988. *On Account of Sex: The Politics of Women's Issues, 1945 to 1968*. Berkeley: University of California Press.

Hartmann, Susan M. 1989. *From Margin to Mainstream*. Philadelphia: Temple University Press.

Heard, Alexander. 1960. *The Costs of Democracy*. Chapel Hill: University of North Carolina Press.

Herndon, James F. 1982. "Access, Record and Competition as Influences on Interest Groups' Contributions to Congressional Campaigns." *Journal of Politics* 44: 996–1019.

Herrnson, Paul S. 1988. *Party Campaigning in the 1980s*. Cambridge, Mass.: Harvard University Press.

Hinich, Melvin J., and Peter C. Ordeshook. 1970. "Plurality Maximization vs. Vote Maximization: A Spatial Analysis with Variable Participation." *American Political Science Review* 64: 772–91.

Hurley, Patricia A. 1982. "Collective Representation Reappraised." *Legislative Studies Quarterly* 7: 119–36.

Jackson, Brooks. 1988. *Honest Graft: Big Money and the American Political Process*. New York: Knopf.

Jacobson, Gary C. 1980. *Money in Congressional Elections*. New Haven: Yale University Press.

_____. 1985. "Money and Votes Reconsidered: Congressional Elections, 1972–1982." *Public Choice* 47: 7–62.

_____. 1985–86. "Party Organization and Distribution of Campaign Resources: Republicans and Democrats in 1982." *Political Science Quarterly* 100: 603–25.

_____. 1987. *The Politics of Congressional Elections*. 2d ed. Glenview, Ill.: Scott Foresman.

_____. 1990. "The Effects of Campaign Spending in House Elections: New Evidence for Old Arguments." *American Journal of Political Science* 34: 334–62.

Jensen, Richard J. 1983. *Grass Roots Politics: Parties, Issues and Voters, 1854–1883*. Westport, Conn: Greenwood Press.

Judge, James B., R. Carter Hill, William Griffiths, Helmut Lutkepohl, and Tsoung-Chao Lee. 1982. *Introduction to the Theory and Practice of Econometrics*. New York: John Wiley.

Kau, James B., Donald Keenan, and Paul H. Rubin. 1982. "A General Equilibrium Model of Congressional Voting." *Quarterly Journal of Economics* 97: 271–93.

Kau, James B., and Paul H. Rubin. 1982. *Congressmen, Constituents and Contributors*. Boston: Martinus Nidjhoff.

Kayden, Xandra, and Eddie Mahe, Jr. 1985. *The Party Goes On*. New York: Basic Books.

Kazee, Thomas A. 1980. "The Decision to Run for the U.S. Congress: Challenger Attitudes in the 1970s." *Legislative Studies Quarterly* 5: 79–100.

Kirkpatrick, Jeane J. 1974. *Political Woman*. New York: Basic Books.

Kleeman, Katherine E. 1983. *Women's PACs*. Rutgers, N.J.: Center for the American Woman and Politics.

Kohn, Walter S. G. 1980. *Women in National Legislatures*. New York: Praeger.

Kousser, J. Morgan. 1974. *The Shaping of Southern Politics*. New Haven: Yale University Press.

Kraditor, Aileen S. 1965. *The Ideas of the Woman Suffrage Movement, 1890–1920.* New York: Columbia University Press.

Langbein, Laura I. 1986. "Money and Access: Some Empirical Evidence." *Journal of Politics* 48: 1052–62.

Latus, Margaret Ann. 1984. "Assessing Ideological PACs: From Outrage to Understanding." In *Money and Politics in the United States*, ed. Michael J. Malbin, pp. 142–71. Chatham, N.J.: Chatham House.

Lawson, Steven F. 1976. *Black Ballots: Voting Rights and the South, 1944–1969.* New York: Columbia University Press.

_____. 1985. *In Pursuit of Power: Southern Blacks and Electoral Politics, 1965–1982.* New York: Columbia University Press.

Leyden, Kevin M., and Stephen A. Borrelli. 1990. "Party Contributions and Party Unity: Can Loyalty be Bought?" *Western Political Quarterly* 43: 343–65.

Luntz, Frank I. 1988. *Candidates, Consultants and Campaigns.* Oxford: Basil Blackwell.

Maddala, G. S. 1983. *Limited-Dependent and Qualitative Variables in Econometrics.* Cambridge: Cambridge University Press.

Magleby, David B., and Candice J. Nelson. 1990. *The Money Chase.* Washington, D.C.: Brookings Institution.

Mandel, Ruth B. 1981. *In the Running: The New Woman Candidate.* Boston: Beacon Press.

Masters, Marick F., and J. T. Delaney. 1985. "The Causes of Union Political Involvement: A Longitudinal Analysis." *Journal of Labor Research* 6: 341–63.

Masters, Marick F., and Gerald D. Keim. 1985. "Determinants of PAC Participation Among Large Corporations." *Journal of Politics* 47: 1150–73.

Meyer, Mary. 1970. "Black Congressmen and How They Grew." *Black Politician* 1: 3–11.

Moe, Terry M. 1980. *The Organization of Interests.* Chicago: University of Chicago Press.

Morris, Milton D. 1984. "Black Electoral Participation and the Distribution of Public Benefits." In *Minority Vote Dilution*, pp. 271–85.

Mueller, Carol. 1986. "Nurturance and Mastery: Competing Qualifications for Women's Access to High Public Office." In *Research in Politics and Society*, ed. Gwen Moore and Glenna Spatz, 2: 211–32.

Mutch, Robert E. 1988. *Campaigns, Congress, and Courts: The Making of Federal Election Campaign Law.* New York: Praeger.

O'Loughlin, John. 1979. "Black Representation Growth and the Seats-Votes Relationship." *Social Science Quarterly* 60: 73–86.

Olson, Mancur. 1965. *The Logic of Collective Action.* Cambridge: Harvard University Press.

Overacker, Louise. 1932. *Money in Elections.* New York: Macmillan.

Parker, Frank R. 1984. "Racial Gerrymandering and Legislative Reapportionment." In *Minority Vote Dilution*, ed. Chandler Davidson. Washington, D.C.: Howard University Press.

Paul, Chris, and Al Wilhite. 1990. "Rent Seeking Under Varying Cost Structures." *Public Choice* 64: 279–90.

Penniman, Harold R. 1984. "U.S. Elections Really a Bargain." *Public Opinion* 7: 51–53.

Pierce, Patrick A. 1989. "Gender Role and Political Culture: the Electoral Connection." *Women & Politics* 9: 21–46.

Pitkin, Hanna. 1967. *The Concept of Representation*. Berkeley: University of California Press.

Poole, Keith T., and L. Harmon Zeigler. 1985. *Women, Public Opinion, and Politics*. New York: Longman.

Poole, Keith T., Thomas Romer, and Howard Rosenthal. 1987. "The Revealed Preferences of Political Action Committees." *American Economic Review* 77: 298–302.

Prewitt, Kenneth, and Heinz Eulau. 1969. "Political Matrix and Political Representation: Prologomenena to a New Departure for an Old Problem." *American Political Science Review* 63: 427–41.

Ragsdale, Lynn, and T. E. Cook. 1987. "Representatives' Actions and Challengers' Reactions: Limits to Candidate Connections in the House." *American Journal of Political Science* 31: 45–81.

Rodine, Sharon. 1990. "How to Beat 'Bubba.' " *Campaigns & Elections* 11 (October/November): 56–57.

Rupp, Leila J., and Verta Taylor. 1987. *Survival in the Doldrums: The American Women's Rights Movement, 1945 to the 1960s*. New York: Oxford University Press.

Sabato, Larry J. 1981. *The Rise of Political Consultants*. New York: Basic Books.

_____. 1984. *PAC Power*. New York: Norton.

_____. 1989. *Paying for Elections*. New York: Priority Press.

Salmore, Barbara G., and Stephen A. Salmore. 1989. *Candidates, Parties, and Campaigns*. 2d ed. Washington, D.C.: CQ Press.

Sapiro, Virginia. 1981. "Research Frontier Essay: When are Interests Interesting? The Problem of Political Representation of Women." *American Political Science Review* 75: 701–16.

Schlesinger, Joseph A. 1975. "The Primary Goals of Political Parties: A Clarification of Positive Theory." *American Political Science Review* 69: 840–49.

_____. 1984. "On the Theory of Party Organization." *Journal of Politics* 46: 369–400.

_____. 1985. "The New American Political Party." *American Political Science Review* 79: 1152–69.

Schroedel, Jean R. 1986. "Campaign Contributions and Legislative Outcomes." *Western Political Quarterly* 39: 371–89.

Scott, Anne Firor. 1970. *The Southern Lady: From Pedestal to Politics, 1830–1930*. Chicago: University of Chicago Press.

Secret, Philip E., and Susan Welch. 1989. "Sex, Race, and Participation: An Analysis of the 1980 and 1984 Elections." *Women & Politics* 9: 57–67.

Shaffer, William R. 1982. "Party and Ideology in the House of Representatives." *Western Political Quarterly* 35: 92–106.

Shepsle, Kenneth A. 1972. "The Strategy of Ambiguity: Uncertainty and Electoral Competition." *American Political Science Review* 66: 555–68.

Shienbaum, Kim E. 1984. *Beyond the Electoral Connection*. Philadelphia: University of Pennsylvania Press.

Shingles, Richard D. 1981. "Black Consciousness and Political Participation: The Missing Link." *American Political Science Review* 75: 76–91.

Sinclair, Barbara. 1990. "The Congressional Party: Evolving Organizational, Agenda-Setting, and Policy Roles." In *The Parties Respond*, ed. L. Sandy Maisel, pp. 227–48. Boulder, Colo: Westview Press.

Smith, Steven S., and Christopher J. Deering. 1984. *Committees in Congress*. Washington, D.C.: CQ Press.

Sonenshein, Raphael J. 1990. "Can Black Candidates Win Statewide Elections?" *Political Science Quarterly* 105: 219–41.

Sorauf, Frank J. 1984. *What Price PACs?* New York: Twentieth Century Fund.

_____. 1984–85. "Who's in Charge? Accountability in Political Action Committees." *Political Science Quarterly* 99: 591–614.

_____. 1988. *Money in American Elections*. Glenview, Ill.: Scott Foresman.

Stanley, Harold W. 1987. *Voter Mobilization and the Politics of Race*. New York: Praeger.

Stern, Philip M. 1988. *The Best Congress Money Can Buy*. New York: Pantheon Books.

Stigler, George J. 1972. "Economic Competition and Political Competition." *Public Choice* 13: 91–106.

Studenmund, A. H., and Henry J. Cassidy. 1987. *Using Econometrics: A Practical Guide*. Boston: Little, Brown and Co.

Thayer, George. 1973. *Who Shakes the Money Tree?* New York: Simon and Schuster.

Theil, Henri. 1971. *Principles of Econometrics*. New York: John Wiley.

Theilmann, John, and Al Wilhite. 1986. "Differences in Campaign Funds: A Racial Explanation." *Review of Black Political Economy* 15: 45–58.

_____. 1989. "The Determinants of Individuals' Campaign Contributions to Congressional Campaigns." *American Politics Quarterly* 17: 312–31.

Thomas, Scott J. 1989. "Do Incumbent Campaign Expenditures Matter?" *Journal of Politics* 51: 965–76.

Thompson, Joan Hulse. 1985. "Career Convergence: Election of Women and Men to the House of Representatives, 1916–1975." *Women & Politics* 5: 69–90.

Tobin, James. 1958. "Estimation of Relationships for Limited Dependent Variables." *Econometrica* 26: 24–36.

Tollison, Robert D. 1982. "Rent Seeking: A Survey." *Kyklos* 35: 575–602.

Tullock, Gordon. 1980. "Efficient Rent-Seeking." In *Toward a Theory of Rent-Seeking Society*, ed. J. M. Buchanan, R. D. Tollison, and Gordon Tullock, pp. 3–15, College Station, Tex.: Texas A&M Press.

Turner, Julius, and Edward V. Schneier, Jr. 1970. *Party and Constituency: Pressure on Congress*. Baltimore: Johns Hopkins University Press.

Uhlaner, Carol J., and Kay L. Schlozman. 1986. "Candidate Gender and Congressional Campaign Receipts." *Journal of Politics* 48: 30–50.

Verba, Sidney, and Norman H. Nie. 1972. *Participation in America*. New York: Harper and Row.

Waldman, Sidney. 1980. "Majority Leadership in the House of Representatives." *Political Science Quarterly* 95: 373–93.

Walton, Hanes, Jr. 1985. *Invisible Politics*. Albany: State University of New York Press.

Wattenberg, Martin P. 1986. *The Decline of American Political Parties, 1952–1984*. Cambridge: Harvard University Press.

Weisberg, Robert. 1978. "Collective vs. Dyadic Representation." *American Political Science Review* 72: 535–47.

Welch, Susan, and Philip Secret. 1981. "Sex, Race and Political Participation." *Western Political Quarterly* 34: 5–16.

Welch, William P. 1982. "Campaign Contributions and Legislative Voting: Milk Money and Dairy Price Supports." *Western Political Quarterly* 35: 478–95.

Whitby, Kenny J. 1987. "Measuring Congressional Responsiveness to Policy Interests of Black Constituents." *Social Science Quarterly* 68: 367–77.

Wilcox, Clyde. 1988a. "I Owe It All to Me: Candidates' Investments in Their Own Campaigns." *American Politics Quarterly* 16: 266–79.

_____. 1988b. "PACs & Pluralism: Interest Group Formation & Partnership." *Polity* 21: 155–66.

Wilhite, Al. 1988. "Political Parties, Campaign Contributions and Discrimination." *Public Choice* 58: 259–68.

Wilhite, Al, and Chris Paul. 1989. "Corporate Campaign Contributions and Legislative Voting." *Quarterly Review of Economics and Business* 29: 73–85.

Wilhite, Al, and John Theilmann. 1986. "Women, Blacks and PAC Discrimination." *Social Science Quarterly* 67: 283–98.

_____. 1987. "Labor PAC Contributions and Labor Legislation: A Simultaneous Logit Approach." *Public Choice* 53: 267–76.

_____. 1989. "Campaign Contributions by Political Parties: Ideology vs. Winning," *Atlantic Economic Journal* 17: 11–20.

Williams, Eddie N. 1982. "Black Political Progress in the 1970s: The Electoral Arena." In *The New Black Politics*, ed. M. B. Preston, L. J. Henderson, Jr., and P. Puryer, pp. 73–108. New York: Longman.

Williams, Linda. 1987. "Black Political Progress in the 1980s: The Electoral Arena." In *The New Black Politics*, 2d ed., eds. M. B. Preston, L. J. Henderson, Jr., and P. Puryer, pp. 97–135. New York: Longman.

Wittman, Donald. 1973. "Parties as Utility Maximizers." *American Political Science Review* 67: 490–98.

Wolfinger, Raymond E., and Steven J. Rosenstone. 1980. *Who Votes?* New Haven: Yale University Press.

Wright, John R. 1985. "PACs, Contributions, and Roll Calls: An Organizational Perspective." *American Political Science Review* 79: 700–14.

_____. 1990. "Contributions, Lobbying and Committee Voting in the U.S. House of Representatives." *American Political Science Review* 84: 417–38.

Index

ABOUT THE AUTHORS

JOHN THEILMANN is Associate Professor of History and Politics at Converse College in South Carolina. The author of several articles and book chapters, he has managed a congressional campaign and engaged in political consulting in Missouri.

AL WILHITE is Professor of Economics at Georgia Southern University. He has published several articles on the determinants of contributions, their impact on legislative voting, and race and gender differentials. His current interest in rent-seeking has prompted him to begin fleshing out theoretical models for past empirical studies.